ADDITIVE ALERT

Your Guide to Safer Shopping

The essential information about
what's *really* in the food you eat,
which additives to avoid and why

Julie Eady

Additive Alert: Your Guide to Safer Shopping

Published by
Additive Alert Pty Ltd
ACN 108 886 522
Mullaloo WA 6027

www.additivealert.com.au

First Published in 2004
Reprinted 2004, 2005, 2005, 2005, 2006
Fully revised July 2006
Reprinted 2006, 2006, 2007, 2007,
Revised 2008
Copyright © Additive Alert Pty Ltd 2004

ISBN 0-9775176-1-6

Cover Design by *Colorlogic*, Ellenbrook WA
Photo courtesy of Community Newspaper Ltd
Printed by *Success Print*, Bayswater WA

Julie Eady is a full time Mum to three young children. She developed her interest in food additives and their effects on health after the birth of her first child. With a family history of allergies and asthma, Julie began her research into dietary links to such illnesses, in an effort to improve her children's chances of avoiding these conditions.

What began as a personal project to identify better food choices for her family, led onto a much bigger project as she discovered the truth about the serious health concerns associated with many additives used in Australian foods.

She is a Director of Additive Alert Pty Ltd, the company she established in 2004 to promote better consumer awareness of food additives and their effects on health, and to advocate for better labelling of Australian foods. In March 2007 Julie was awarded the Western Australian Consumer Protection Award, in recognition of her work as a consumer advocate and the benefits her work with Additive Alert has brought to the community.

Julie lives in Perth with her husband Stuart and children Jaslyn, Mitchell and Jonothan. She enjoys living a healthy life by the beach with holidays back to the Kimberley to escape the winter chills as often as possible.

Disclaimer

This book has been compiled from the author's own research and personal experiences. The content is not intended to constitute scientific or medical advice or to include all information about all additives used in food. Every effort has been made to ensure that the information contained in this book is accurate and current at the time of publication.

Numerous existing public references were consulted and cross-referenced in preparing this book and in determining the health risks attributed to certain additives. The author does not guarantee the accuracy of the information obtained from the sources or cited references and disclaims liability for the accuracy of that information. The author also does not endorse, recommend or promote any product over another.

The author acknowledges that product content may change from time to time and welcomes product updates for any products cited in this book so that any omissions, errors or additive changes can be corrected in future editions.

Additive Alert: Your Guide to Safer Shopping is intended to enable readers to form their own judgments about which products best suit their individual needs. The author disclaims liability for any use, misuse or misunderstanding of any information contained herein, or for any loss, damage or injury (be it health, financial or otherwise) for any individual or group acting upon or relying on information contained in or inferred from this work.

A qualified health practitioner should always be consulted about individuals' health requirements and any significant dietary changes.

Acknowledgements

There are many people who have helped to make this book a reality. The idea for this work first glimmered in 2002, and it has taken me two-and-a-half years since then to finish the project, in between looking after my daughter, being pregnant again and welcoming Mitchell into our family. This wouldn't have been possible without a lot of help from my wonderful family.

My special thanks go to my husband Stuart and my daughter Jaslyn, for their love and understanding and the time off to lock myself in the office and to spend countless hours in the supermarket surveying product ingredients.

My thanks also go to the rest of my family — Jocelyn, Mark, Helen, Ross and Helen — for their unwavering encouragement and support of my idea, their positive contributions and suggestions, and mostly for their babysitting.

A special thanks goes to Mark and Vaughan for their technical help and advice.

I'd also like to thank Dr Peter Dingle for being so generous with his time and expertise. His enthusiasm and encouragement gave me the inspiration to believe that small steps taken by ordinary people can make a big difference, and the courage to ensure that this book was finished.

I hope it makes a difference in some small way to the health and wellbeing of others.

Foreword

Have you ever wondered why we have increasing rates of childhood illness despite the increasing amounts of money we put into our health system? Do you wonder why rates of cancer, ADHD, depression, suicide and even cardiovascular disease continue to rise in children? The reason is clear. We do not have a system that creates health. We have a pharmaceutical-based health system that treats the symptoms and not the disease.

In Australia each month 60000 prescriptions for antidepressants are written out for people under 20 years of age, and this is on the increase.

If we had a health system, it would be targeting our poor Diets, our contaminated Environment, our negative Attitude and our stressed Lifestyle. Something I call the DEAL, rather than prescribing medications that have serious side effects and, at best, only short-term benefits.

If you are interested in good health, where do you start? I suggest you look at what you put in your mouth, particularly the food additives.

Many food additives are cosmetic ingredients used for the sole purpose of fooling the consumer. Did you know that most have no benefit and many have serious adverse effects? Research over the past 40 years has linked many of the artificial food colours derived from petrol with ADHD and certain allergic reactions. The chemicals that form the preservatives put into processed meats definitely cause cancer and are directly linked with childhood leukaemia. This scares me because I see many children eating lots of processed meats in the form of luncheon meats, sausages, frankfurts and party sausages.

On top of this, the foods containing most of these additives are targeted to the most vulnerable group in our population, our children. Children are much more vulnerable because their bodies are growing and laying down their foundation for health for the rest of their lives. Numerous studies have shown children react more severely to many of these toxic food additives than adults.

Yet, every year, food manufacturers target advertising at youth, to fool them into believing that these over-processed foods with lots of additives and no nutrition are going to bring some benefit - either social, psychological, emotional or physical. Have you ever wondered why you never see a really obese group of kids with ADHD and depression on a soft drink or lolly advertisement?

You need to know the hard facts about food additives and that they are a significant contributing factor to our kids' poor health.

My utopia in the future will not put our kids' health at risk. Future governments will put our health first and economics second. Governments will not allow substances to be added to foods unless they benefit our kids and add some nutrition, and industry will substitute beneficial additives and go back to putting real food in our food.

But until such a utopia arrives, you need to learn as much as you can about food additives and change what you can in your own lives. Do this by reading this book.

Dr Peter Dingle
Environmental and Nutritional Toxicologist
School of Environmental Science
Murdoch University
www.drdingle.com

Author of
The DEAL for Happier, Healthier, Smarter Kids: A Twenty First Century Guide for Parents

Contents

Introduction

Most people want to be healthy and avoid disease and illness. Most parents, in particular, want their children to be healthy and safe and wouldn't dream of intentionally feeding or exposing them to dangerous chemicals or toxins. Unfortunately, most of us have little idea about the chemicals and toxins we're exposed to every day in our environment, and worse, through the food we eat.

The following examples may shock you, but — incredibly — they are real.

- Many brands of peanut butter in Australia contain a particularly nasty chemical known as butylated hydroxyanisole (BHA). This chemical is known to cause stomach cancer in rats and mice and is strongly thought to be a human carcinogen also. Usually there's no mention of this additive on the label due to a loophole in the labelling laws in this country. Other equally effective, non-toxic additives exist that can do the same job, but BHA is cheaper and so is more widely used.

- Ice cream cones, you'd think, wouldn't contain many additives, and, if they did, surely they would be non-toxic? Think again. Most popular brands contain at least three artificial colours that are linked to hyperactivity, are suspected or known carcinogens that are banned in the US, and/or are known mutagens (agents that damage DNA). In addition, many of these products also contain the antioxidant BHA, mentioned above.

- Baby food is protected under legislation from the addition of many of the more toxic common food additives. Even so, throughout the research for this book, examples were found of well-known baby foods that contained suspected carcinogens, mutagens, and artificial colours that are known to promote hyperactivity and are linked to asthma.

There are many more disturbing examples of toxic chemicals in the food we eat everyday, some of which I will share with you throughout this book. These "additives" aren't food–they are toxic chemicals–and they have no place in our diet.

Many food additives are harmless and may be beneficial, but there are numerous food additives still in use today that are known to be dangerous and which, given the choice, most of us would choose not to consume or feed to our families.

You are probably thinking, "How can this be true? Surely it's illegal in Australia to put toxic chemicals in the food we buy?" Unfortunately, it isn't. Of the 300 or so permitted food additives in Australia at least 30 are *known or suspected carcinogens*. Many others are banned in other countries because of known adverse health effects, yet are still permitted in Australia.

The reason for this is that our testing of food chemicals isn't as rigorous as in other countries. In some countries, a food additive will be banned if it's seen to cause any cancerous effects in any animal studies.

In Australia, astoundingly, this precautionary principle isn't applied universally when evaluating the safety of food additives. This is why we have carcinogenic, mutagenic and teratogenic substances (agents that can cause birth defects) present quite legally in many of our processed foods today. More about this and the regulation of food additives in Australia can be found in *Chapter 6: Testing and approval of additives* on page 22.

Despite all this, however, there's some very good news. There still are many low additive, healthier choices available in our supermarkets today. Even with the ever increasing prevalence of food additives in our food, across most product ranges there are smart choices that the informed shopper can make.

We can greatly reduce our daily intake of unnecessary, and often unsafe, food chemicals and toxins simply by choosing products that don't contain these dangerous substances. Thankfully, there are still products with little or no "nasty" additives in them, and these are the products we should be supporting.

The food-manufacturing industry is big business. There is a vast amount of energy and money invested by the food industry into packaging goods to be appealing to customers. In some cases, downright misleading and false statements are made to reassure consumers about the safety of products. For example, undesirable ingredients are listed using long and complex chemical names and numbers, or are simply not declared at all.

The reality is, that although most people would like to be better informed about the food they eat and what is in it, most of us can't find the time to read and understand food labels. The people who most often do are the people who have to — usually those with a health problem or those with a child or family member with an illness or health concern. Most of us are simply too busy to take on this task and we assume and hope that the food we buy must be safe. Unfortunately this isn't always the case, even in Australia.

But relax, keep reading and don't panic!

You don't have to become a label-reading expert or a dedicated home scientist to decipher all the chemical names, numbers and symbols, to eliminate many of these suspect chemicals from your family's diet.

Additive Alert: Your Guide to Safer Shopping has been compiled to put you, the consumer, back in control of what you buy and what you put into your body. With a little bit of knowledge about how to read food labels, and up-to-date information about which additives you need to avoid, you can very easily make some simple changes to your shopping and eating habits that will reap real benefits for your whole family.

In the following pages you'll learn how to avoid products with suspect additive ingredients. Armed with this information you can greatly reduce your consumption of these chemicals and, most likely, improve your health in the process.

Chapter 1: About this book

1.1 Introduction

This book is designed to be a practical shoppers' guide that will inform consumers about the possible health risks associated with many food additives, and how to select the best, low-additive products commonly available in our major supermarkets.

It has been compiled using the most up-to-date references about food additives and is intended to give you, the consumer, the information you need to decide which additives you wish to avoid.

Not all additives are bad or harmful, so it doesn't follow that the product with the least additives is necessarily the best. *Additive Alert: Your Guide to Safer Shopping* will tell you which additives are considered harmful or suspect, and will tell you how to read the labels so you'll know what's in the products you're buying and can choose the products with the least amount of harmful additives.

Imagine you're buying potato chips for your kids. You may think there's very little difference across brands, but when it comes to additives, there are some big differences. For example:

> The ingredients panel of brand A potato chips lists only one additive: *antioxidant 319.*
>
> The ingredients panel of brand B potato chips lists two additives: *antioxidant 304* and *306.*

After reading this book you'll know to choose brand B.

Why? Because antioxidant 319 is one of the nastiest food additives and should be avoided, especially by children. It's known to cause cancer and birth defects in animals, and a dose of just 5 grams is fatal to an adult human. Antioxidants 304 and 306, however, are perfectly safe, beneficial additives, with no known health risks.

So although brand A has only one additive, it's one you most definitely want to avoid. Armed with this knowledge, most of us would choose brand B and probably decide to never eat brand A again.

After reading this book, you'll have all the information you need to decide which additives you wish to avoid. *Additive Alert: Your Guide to Safer Shopping* will tell you which additives are linked to asthma, cancer and hyperactivity. You will also learn which additives aren't recommended for children and pregnant women, and which additives are actually *prohibited* in children's foods because of their known adverse health risks. The guide also highlights additives that are *banned in other countries* because of their adverse health risks, and those not recommended for people with kidney or liver complaints or salicylate-intolerance problems.

It isn't intended for this book to be viewed as a definitive scientific reference. It is primarily an information booklet and a shoppers' guide to help consumers avoid additives they don't wish to consume.

What is provided here is a compilation of current information about the known, or suspected, adverse health effects of some food additives. This information has been sourced from a range of existing credible references as cited in the references starting on page 137.

1.2   What this book tells you and what it doesn't

This book will not tell you what specific products to buy, and it doesn't recommend any particular brand over another. That is for each of us to determine depending upon our tastes, budgets and health needs.

The book only refers to additive content and doesn't rate any other nutritional considerations such as fat, salt or fibre content.

Once again, these are individual concerns that vary from person to person. In some cases, for example, the "best" choice from an additive perspective may not be the best choice in relation to fat content for you. It is up to each of us to select the products overall that meet our needs best.

However, it's a general observation that those products with few or no undesirable additives tend to be the better quality choices all round. Many of the worst additives are often found in lower quality foodstuffs.

Often these additives are cheaper processing aids, or they are additives used to bulk up food or, in some cases, to improve poor flavour. So you'll find, in general, that the foods with the worst additive contents are often the poorer choices healthwise and tastewise. Still, they sometimes win out as the cheapest option.

This book will give you a basic understanding of what food additives are and what they are used for, and also the regulation of food additives in Australia.

It will explain to you how to read labels and will reveal the loopholes in our labelling system, and how to spot hidden additives when selecting your groceries.

It will highlight for you which additives are particularly nasty and should be avoided and why.

It will also give you some practical hints about how to modify your eating and shopping habits, to significantly and easily reduce the amount of unnecessary and unsafe food additives you and your family consume every day.

If you want more details about individual additives, this book also provides you with a detailed list of all permitted additives in Australia and their potential health impacts to keep and use as a reference.

In addition, this book provides you with some very useful contacts and links for further information, if you want to know more.

Chapter 2: Food additives: what and why?

2.1 Introduction

So what exactly are food additives? A food additive isn't a food in itself, but is defined as *any substance that is added to food to achieve a technological function.* A technological function could be anything from improving colour or taste, preserving the food, preventing rancidity or improving the texture or appearance of the food.

In Australia, there are approximately 300 substances permitted under the Food Standards Australia New Zealand (FSANZ) guidelines. Many additives are necessary and beneficial in that they stop food from decaying, prevent bacteria and other contaminants, or they genuinely improve the food in a beneficial way.

Other additives, however, are added purely for cosmetic purposes and, in some cases, to fool the consumer. For example:

- Vibrant colours are added to appeal to children.

- Flavour enhancers are used to give extra taste to otherwise tasteless products.

- Thickeners are added to make watered-down products seem more substantial.

These types of additives aren't necessary but are used at the *manufacturers'* discretion, and are often just a means of disguising substandard foods that would otherwise not taste or look appealing.

A food additive may be from a natural source such as vitamin C (additive 300), or it may be entirely synthetic and produced by chemical processes. Just because some additives are from a natural source originally doesn't mean that these additives are any safer than their chemical cousins. Manufacturers, though, often play heavily on the term *natural* because it sounds much safer and more appealing than *artificial.*

Food additives in Australia are classified by the functions they perform. An additive may perform different functions in different products, and its function must be declared on the label. In Australia, an additive must be declared to perform a *technological function* to be permitted.

Incredibly, though, it's the *manufacturer's* discretion, not that of FSANZ, the regulatory authority, that determines what, if any, technological function is being performed.

Take, for example, green tomato sauce. This is made green by adding in Curcumin 100, Tartrazine 102 (linked to hyperactivity, migraines, skin irritations, sleep disorders) and Brilliant Blue 133 (a suspected carcinogen and linked to hyperactivity). It could be argued that the only "function" of making tomato sauce green is to increase the marketing appeal to kids — hardly a necessary technological function. Nonetheless, it's totally legal under the current guidelines.

2.2   The functions of food additives

The various functions that food additives perform, beneficial or cosmetic, are as follows:

Anti-caking agents

These reduce the tendency of individual food particles to adhere and clump.

Anti-foaming agents

These prevent excessive frothing or scum forming when food is boiled.

Antioxidants

These prevent oxidation, which can lead to rancidity and colour changes.

Bleaching agents

These are used to whiten flours.

Bulking agents

These contribute to the volume of food without affecting its energy content. They are often used in low-joule food where sugar is being replaced.

Colourings

These add or restore colour to foods.

Emulsifiers

These prevent oil-and-water mixtures from separating.

Firming agents, stabilisers

These maintain the uniform dispersion of substances in solid and semi-solid food.

Flavour enhancers

These enhance the existing taste or odour of a food.

Flour-treatment agents

These improve the colour or baking quality of flour and stimulate yeast activity.

Food acids

These help to maintain a constant acid level.

Glazing agents

These are used to give food a shiny appearance and/or a protective coating.

Humectants

These help to prevent food from drying out.

Mineral salts

These are added to improve texture or water-holding capacity. They can increase plumpness and help firmness.

Preservatives

These retard or prevent spoilage by inhibiting micro-organisms.

Propellants

These are used in aerosol cans to expel the contents.

Sweetening agents

These replace the sweetness normally provided by sugars without contributing significantly to the overall energy content.

Vegetable gums

These are all derived from plant sources and help improve the texture of foods.

2.3 Additive numbers

In Australia, the food-additive code numbers are the same as those adopted by the European Economic Community. In Europe, all additives are assigned an E number; for example, E621 is MSG.

In Australia we use the same numbers but we don't use the E prefix. MSG thus appears on Australian labels as MSG or just 621.

2.4 Additives explosion

People have been adding substances to food for centuries to help preserve and improve its taste. The original food additives were substances such as smoke, spices, salt, sugar, vinegar and salt petre. Over time, and with the proliferation of highly refined and processed foods, more food additives have been developed and utilised by the food industry.

Not that long ago, people ate mainly fresh foods in season and cooked things from scratch. We baked cakes and biscuits and made sauces, stews and gravies. The typical western diet of today relies extensively on packaged, highly processed, highly refined foods. Consumers today are demanding more and more variety. We expect food to last and to enjoy foods that aren't local or in season. We are also demanding that food is quick, easy and even "instant" in some cases.

Such expectations can only be met through the greatly increased use of food additives. As a result, we're consuming more and more additives in our day-to-day lives. It is estimated that the average Australian adult consumes at least *5 kilograms* of food additives each year. Most of us would have no idea what sorts of chemicals and toxins that 5 kilograms contains and what the potential health effects could be. If we did know, many of us would be horrified.

Today, most additives found in our foods are safe and well tested, but more and more additives are being developed and included in our food supply as manufacturers compete for our shopping dollar. Over the past century, many additives have been permitted and used in our food supply and then banned as their adverse health effects later became apparent. In these cases, the adverse health effects have only been proven *after* the additive has been in circulation for a considerable time, often decades. Only then is the real health impact on humans discernable and the additive recalled.

Unfortunately, there are still numerous additives currently permitted and widely used in our food supply that are poorly tested or, in some cases, known to be harmful and which should definitely be avoided.

Not everybody, however, is concerned about the connection between food additives and adverse health effects. Let's have a look at what the issues are surrounding the use of food additives and our health.

Chapter 3: Additives and health concerns

3.1 A picture of health

Consider for a moment the following snapshot of the health of our society in 2008:

- The incidence of asthma is increasing almost all over the world, and experts don't know why (1).[†] In Australia, we have one of the highest asthma rates in the world with 14.7% of Australians being asthmatic. One in four Australian children suffer from chronic asthma, and half as many again suffer from regular wheezing and asthma-like symptoms. Asthma is the most common cause of hospital admissions among children.

- A 2002 Federal government survey into mental health identified 11.2% of Australia's children as suffering from ADD or ADHD. Additional research showed that 1 in 50 Australian children were on medication such as dexamphetamine to control ADHD. In Western Australia, these drugs are being prescribed at a rate of nearly four times the national average (2), and it's estimated that at least one child in every classroom can be expected to be taking this type of medication.

- Teen suicide rates for males have quadrupled since the 1960s, along with a shocking increase in mental health problems for today's youth. One in five Australian adolescents is estimated to have significant mental health problems, and 15% have behavioural problems that interfere with learning (3).

- More kids are getting brain cancer. The diagnosis of brain tumours has increased a whopping 21% over the past five years and continues to rise (4). In fact, after injuries and violence, cancer is the leading cause of death in American children (5).

[†]   Numbers in brackets refer to the sources listed at the end of the chapter.

- Cancer rates in general continue to skyrocket. Currently more than one third of all of us will develop cancer in our lifetime and one fourth will die from the disease (6).

- There's been an alarming increase in the reported incidence of cancer among young children and adolescents, especially brain cancer, testicular cancer and acute lymphocytic leukaemia over the past 50 years (7).

- Obesity is becoming our number one national health crisis. One in four Australian children is overweight or obese. A 2003 survey into obesity by health fund HBF revealed that childhood obesity in Australia continues to rise at a rate of one per cent per year. If this continues, half of all young Australians will be obese by 2025.

- The rate of diabetes in Australia has almost doubled in the past five years. It is the world's fastest growing disease and the sixth biggest killer in Australia. Today 5% of Australians have diabetes, and the incidence of both type-1 and type-2 diet-related diabetes is increasing rapidly amongst both children and adults (8). Once regarded as an adult disease, type-2 (or lifestyle diabetes) is now being seen in children as young as eight because of the escalating obesity rates affecting our kids (9).

- According to the Heart Research Institute, heart disease is now Australia's biggest killer, and around 40% of Australian children are now showing early signs of heart disease by the age of 15.

And this is the lucky country!

We *are* lucky in that we have excellent diagnosis and access to treatment options, but this is not reducing the incidence of these crippling conditions. Statistics like these are sending us a very clear message – unless something changes dramatically we are facing a fairly bleak future on the health front. What is even more alarming and indisputable is the fact that we have a *child health crisis* on our hands in Australia. We cannot ignore the grim prediction now being made by many eminent and reputable professionals that this generation of children is the first generation of children likely to die before their parents.

So what can we do? For more and more people worldwide, including an ever growing number of health professionals, the path towards arresting these alarming trends lies in prevention, not treatment of the symptoms once disease is already well entrenched. When we start to focus on prevention, this is where commonsense tells us that we need to look closely at *all* contributing factors, including diet.

3.2   So what's going on?

Many factors are contributing to the mental and physical health problems that are becoming so entrenched in western society that they are beginning to be seen as the norm. For a child to suffer from asthma or be diagnosed with ADD or ADHD today isn't rare as the previous statistics clearly demonstrate.

It wasn't always this way, was it?

Think back to when you went to school. How many kids did you know with asthma? Were obese or overweight children a common sight? Sure, there were a few high-spirited ratbags in every school — the ones who were always in trouble — but was one in every five kids clinically depressed or suffering from behavioural or learning problems? It didn't seem that way to me.

Better diagnosis and community awareness of chronic conditions such as cancer, asthma, diabetes and behavioural disorders can definitely help explain some of the rising incidence of all these serious ailments. Many professionals argue, though, that it cannot *all* be put down to just better diagnosis.

So what has changed?

The answer is a lot has changed, and very quickly, but two factors in particular are most regarded as having the biggest impact on our current health.

First, our environment has changed. We are now being exposed to environmental toxins at previously unimaginable concentrations. Unless you live in a sterile bubble, you're exposed to an unbelievable cocktail of environmental toxins in every facet of your life, and have been since before you were born.

Today's breast milk still contains toxic remnants of DDT and other toxic chemicals banned many years ago. These agents are known to cause cancer, deformities, physical and mental problems, and are being passed along from grandmother to mother to child. Pesticides, fertilisers, household and industrial chemicals pervade every aspect of daily lives. From the pesticide residues in food, to the toxins in the air we breathe, the water we drink and the products we use in our homes and on our bodies, it's all just one big chemical cocktail, the ongoing combination effect of which is unknown.

Second, our diet has changed dramatically. The past century has seen a phenomenal increase in the demand for processed and refined foods. This has led to a dramatic change in the way we eat and what's in the food we eat. Although the typical diet of 50 years ago would likely be considered too high in saturated fats by today's standards, it may well have been healthier overall as it contained a much higher ratio of natural, unprocessed, chemically unaltered food than the average diet today.

3.3 Could it be the food?

In the 1970s, a US researcher, Dr Ben Feingold, developed a diet free of synthetic colourings, preservatives and naturally occurring salicylates that became known as the Feingold diet. It was designed to assist primarily in the management of hyperactive children, and its introduction heralded a new awareness about the link between food additives and health problems.

Since then, the debate about the effect of food additives on health has continued strongly. Ongoing research and scrutiny is showing substantial scientific and anecdotal links between the growing use of certain food additives in our over-processed diets, and the explosion of a multitude of physical and behavioural health problems in our society.

For example:

- Many food colourings are known or suspected carcinogens and mutagens, and many are known to elicit hyperactivity.

- Many preservatives, especially the sulphites, are known to be dangerous to asthmatics, whilst another group of very common preservatives, the propionates, are now associated with the development of behavioural and learning impairment symptoms. Some common antioxidants are linked to cancer and asthma development.

- Flavour enhancers are implicated in a range of serious health impacts including nausea, restlessness, skin complaints, migraines, sleeping problems, terrible rashes, behaviour and learning problems. Most recently these additives are also being queried in relation to obesity and depression, two of the biggest threats facing this generation of children.

- Other additives are prohibited for use in infants' and children's food, and some are thought to cause damage *in utero* and should be avoided by pregnant and breast feeding women.

3.4 Food allergies and food intolerance

When we talk about the effect of food additives, it isn't suggested that the food we buy in the supermarkets containing colours and antioxidants will make you keel over instantly or trigger a violent and obvious reaction. What more and more people are realising, though, is that it's the *long-term, cumulative, subtle* effects of these food additives in our diets that we need to be concerned about.

Not everyone is affected by food additives in the same way. Some people have true food allergies, while an ever-increasing number of people are developing food intolerances and chemical sensitivities that manifest in many different ways.

Most people, however, are unaware that their overall physical and mental health may be impacted by the common side effects of many food additives. Equally, most people are unaware that their health and general wellbeing may be greatly improved by the removal of common food additives from their diet.

True food allergies are quite rare. Only 1% of adults are estimated to be affected, but up to 5% of children are allergic, and this rate is increasing dramatically every year. True allergic reactions typically manifest in immediate and drastic symptoms including anaphylaxis, which can result in death. Common allergens include cows' milk, eggs, peanuts, shellfish, wheat, soy and nuts.

Food intolerance, however, is very different, much more common and also on the increase. Officially, about 10% of the population is estimated to suffer from food intolerance, but that estimate is growing rapidly every year for two reasons. First, more and more people are coming to understand that food intolerance may be contributing to their symptoms. Ailments and symptoms previously put down to environment or genetics are now being successfully managed and alleviated through diet modification. Second, our over-exposure to chemicals and toxins in both our environment and food is causing more people to become sensitised, and this is manifesting in rising numbers of people with food and other chemical sensitivity problems.

Food intolerance differs greatly from food allergies, and it's a complex subject. Food intolerance reactions can be many and varied and can be triggered by food additives or natural chemicals in food. Reactions can be delayed and very subtle, manifesting as chronic and lingering complaints such as skin disorders, headaches, sleep disturbances, behavioural problems or gastric complaints.

Food intolerance is also dose related, and children are more susceptible because, dose for weight, they consume a higher dose of food chemicals than adults. Food intolerance is strongly associated with behaviour and learning problems as well as varied physical symptoms and can only be diagnosed though careful and supervised elimination diets.

For more information on food intolerance refer to "Fed Up" by Sue Dengate.

3.5   Sources

1.   Sue Dengate, *"Fed Up with Asthma"*; 2003

2.   Commonwealth Department Health and Aged Care, Australian Bureau of Statistics 2000

3.   Prof Fiona Stanley, Director, Institute of Child Health Research, Perth; *"Children in Crisis: Expert"*; The West Australian Nov 2002, *"A battle plan to save the children of a toxic society"*; The Australian, 2002

4.   Australian Institute of Health Welfare, Australian Bureau of Statistics

5.   Mount Sinai School of Medicine, Centre for Children's Health and Environment; *"More kids are getting brain cancer. Why?"*

6.   Dr Samuel S Epstein, Cancer Prevention Coalition; *"Unreasonable Risk"*; 2002

7.   Mount Sinai School of Medicine, Centre for Children's Health and Environment; *"More kids are getting brain cancer. Why?"*

8.   Diabetes Australia

9.   Medical Journal of Australia–Report by Princess Margaret Hospital, May 2004

Chapter 4: Your health, your choice

The important thing to realise is that food intolerance and the effect of food additives aren't just an issue for those with chronic health ailments, colicky babies, hyperactive kids or children suffering behavioural problems. These are the more obvious reactions in those people who react to lower doses, but we're *all* consuming these additives in ever increasing amounts.

Just because these additives don't appear to cause an immediate effect in ourselves, doesn't mean there's no effect. What effect is being had on the inside? What will the cumulative effect be on our bodies in 15 or 20 years time?

Many people are only aware of the most obvious, well-known effects of food additives. Parents often comment about kids going "hyper" after red cordial or a junk-food binge at birthday parties, but most don't regard these effects as a serious health impact. If parents knew that the colours, preservatives and flavour enhancers that elicit these behavioural changes are also, in many cases, carcinogens, mutagens and neural toxins that may cause long-term adverse effects on their children's health, many would be appalled.

For example, because I know that Brilliant Blue (133) is a suspected carcinogen, I choose not to eat it, and definitely make sure I don't feed it regularly to my children. Most people and most parents, I am sure, will not choose products containing suspected carcinogens or other known toxins for their family if they can help it. The sad fact is that most people have no idea at all that these additives aren't good for us.

A growing number of people are aware of safety concerns about food additives and make an effort to steer clear of the most obvious suspects such as bright colours, MSG and artificial sweeteners. What many people don't realise is the unbelievable proliferation of less obvious, but equally harmful, additives throughout our food.

Once it was mainly the obvious junk and fast foods that contained the worst suspect additives, but the use of these additives in everyday "healthy" foods is becoming solidly entrenched.

Preservatives, colours and flavour enhancers are commonly found in margarines. Aspartame is being put in sausages and yoghurts, and chocolate biscuits are made beautifully brown by the use of red, blue, yellow and green colours. Every day it's getting harder and harder to avoid food additives as their use becomes more and more widespread.

Most people don't want to know all the details; they just want to know what's safe and what's not. Unfortunately, it's not always that easy, but the bottom line is this: *many additives in use in our foods today are, at least questionable and, at worst, known to be toxic.*

As consumers, we cannot rely on regulating authorities and especially not food manufacturing companies to safeguard our health. They both have too many vested interests — the most obvious one being money.

History has shown that many additives have previously passed laboratory tests and been permitted, only to be recalled and banned years later as obvious adverse effects in humans became apparent. Food scientists estimate that it takes about 30 years to properly monitor and evaluate the effects of a new additive in circulation in the human population. Many people are now choosing not to be the unwitting guinea pigs in these tests. Many additives are poorly tested and more information is needed, but there's enough information around today for us all to become empowered and make sensible choices about the food we eat.

As parents, it's even more important to know which additives need to be avoided and to keep these out of our children's diets as much as possible. Children need good nutrition and clean environments to allow them to develop physically, mentally and emotionally in the way that nature intended. They don't need daily doses of chemicals, stimulants and toxins.

Generally people don't want to be strictly puritan about the food they eat unless they have to, and sadly, most people will not make serious diet changes until their health is already impacted. The good news is it really isn't that hard to take control. By gaining a little bit of knowledge and shopping wisely, you can make some very significant, very smart changes to the foods you eat and the foods you avoid. These can greatly enhance the health of yourself and your family.

So much is not known about the effect of chemicals and additives in our food. Those wanting to promote additives will discredit research that shows adverse effects in animals, saying that animal tests don't necessarily translate to humans. Those on the other side of the fence will argue that any adverse effects in animals must be interpreted as being relevant to humans as a precautionary measure.

The reality is that it's up to each of us to make our own decisions and choices about the food we eat. What we should remember though, is that even if these suspect additives can never be proven to cause the ill effects in humans that they cause in animal studies, they will never be proven to be doing us any good.

> Good, fresh, real food does us good, and that is what we should be trying to eat.

Chapter 5: Regulation in Australia

The use of food additives in Australia is governed by the Food Standards Code and regulated by Food Standards Australia New Zealand (FSANZ). Their charter is to protect the health and safety of the people of Australia and New Zealand by maintaining a safe food supply.

The official line in relation to food additives, from the Federal Minister down, is *"If it's approved for use in Australia then it's safe"*. This is the response you'll get if you ring FSANZ and ask them anything about any food additive currently approved for use in Australia.

In my initial research into this matter I had numerous discussions with well meaning and helpful staff at FSANZ, but I was unable to get any satisfactory answers to my questions. For example:

(My questions are shown below in bold. FSANZ responses are shown in italics.)

Why in Australia do we have additives that are prohibited in other countries as suspected or known carcinogens?

Different countries have different approval systems. Some countries ban products if they cause DNA changes at any level in any animal ... just because something causes cancer in rats and mice doesn't mean it will cause cancer in humans...

Can you provide me with a list of food additives that have been previously permitted and subsequently withdrawn because of health and/or safety concerns?

No. We don't have a database with that sort of safety information on it. There is no way of collating that sort of information–some additives have been recalled in the past for a variety of reasons but you can't get a list of them...

Can you tell me if there are any health or safety concerns associated with any permitted food additives?

No. Anything which is approved for use in Australia, is considered safe, so we cannot provide any information about any supposed safety concerns. If it's approved, it's safe ...

But what about something like Amaranth (123) — a banned carcinogen in the US that's still permitted in Australia?

The US has a different system — all additives permitted in Australia are considered safe whether or not they are banned overseas. I can't comment on other countries' systems...

Why, if some additives are prohibited in foods for infants and young children, are they present in foods such as chips, corn chips and cheese snacks, which are directly marketed at the children?

By definition, FSANZ regards infants and young children as under 12 months. Therefore, additives such as 621 and 635 are permitted in these foods, as they are not regarded as foods, which would be expected to be marketed directly to, or consumed by those under 12 months....

S

It seems that FSANZ isn't interested in any discussion about the safety or potential adverse health effects of food additives: *"If it's approved, it's safe"*. In other words, "Don't you worry about that. We're here to look after you".

Unfortunately, after my attempts to inform myself via FSANZ, I was not reassured. I was very worried.

It is not acceptable that we have additives in our food that are recognised internationally as suspected or known carcinogens. These additives are banned in other countries, or widely linked to other serious adverse health impacts, yet FSANZ permits them in our food.

I had always assumed that Australia would be one of the more progressive countries in matters such as this. Didn't you? Well, incredibly, this isn't so.

I had also assumed that the regulatory authority would be the best place to locate up-to-date, accurate information about food additives and their effects.

Wrong again.

Although I'm sure FSANZ has lots of up-to-date information about the known and potential effects of food additives, apparently this isn't data that they are willing to give to us, the consumers.

From my research, it appears that most Australians are unaware of the shortcomings of our regulatory body. Most people (quite rightly) assume and expect that the regulatory authority is regulating stringently on their behalf. Unfortunately, it seems that FSANZ isn't able to meet this basic and reasonable expectation.

Try it for yourself, and see what level of information you can access from FSANZ to help you make informed decisions about what you eat. Their contact details are listed in *Appendix 3: Useful contacts* on page 106.

Chapter 6: Testing and approval of additives

6.1 The current system

FSANZ's standard response to any query about the safety of food additives has been that all additives are stringently tested before being allowed in Australia, and are only allowed in levels considered safe. This may be true, but is it good enough? Unfortunately, what is considered safe isn't a universal concept, and the regulation of and attitudes towards food additives varies from country to country.

Before an additive can be approved for use in food in Australia there's a standard application-and-approval process set out by FSANZ. This includes (amongst many other criteria) a requirement that the *manufacturers* provide new or existing scientific evidence to demonstrate the safety of the additive. This information is evaluated — *but not conducted by* —FSANZ scientists, and the additive is subsequently allowed or denied.

Generally, additives are tested initially in two-species animal studies to see if there are any effects on DNA, any links to cancer, major damage to vital organs etc. If any signs of cellular damage (or other untoward effects) are seen at high doses then a *no-observable-effect level* is determined. This is the largest level of additive that has no noticeable effect. An *acceptable daily intake* (ADI) level for people is then set. This is expressed as a dosage per kilogram of body weight, and the quantity of additive likely to be eaten by the vast majority of people must be kept below this acceptable daily intake.

Some additives for which no harmful effects are known have no ADI set, so manufacturers can use these additives in any proportion. Others have very low ADI levels. This indicates that adverse effects were observed in the initial testing on the additive, but the ADI level represents the level of consumption, which is considered safe.

For example, Annatto (160b) has a very low ADI of 0.065 milligrams per kg of body weight, as there are still ongoing queries over the long-term safety of this additive; whereas, beta carotene (160a) has no ADI set as there are no known adverse effects associated with this additive.

6.2   So what's the problem?

There are many shortcomings with the current system of testing, approval and review of additives in Australia. With our current system, additives can be known to cause serious adverse effects at high doses in animal studies, yet small doses throughout our food are considered safe.

There are many additives banned in other countries because of their links to adverse health impacts including cancer, but permitted in Australia at these "safe levels". In other countries, including America, a more stringent precautionary approach is taken, especially in regard to cancer. In America, if any link to cancer exists at any level then the additive isn't permitted.

The concepts of safe levels and acceptable daily intake are questionable too. These are set based on the projected average adult intake. There is no separate ADI set for children, so dose for weight, our kids are getting a much higher dose of these additives than would be intended. Also, many of the more suspect toxic additives with the lowest ADIs are found prolifically in children's foods such as lollies and snack foods. It is doubtful whether the dietary mapping done to set the ADI for general adult consumption would properly reflect what children today are really eating.

There are numerous studies demonstrating the much higher sensitivity to chemical carcinogens of young animals compared to adults. This is due to their limited physiological capability to detoxify carcinogens because of their immature liver enzymes, plus the fact that their cells are dividing more rapidly than adults, increasing the risk of DNA mutations in the cells and the development of delayed cancers in adult life.

The increased susceptibility of infants and young children to a wide range of carcinogens has been fully recognised for well over two decades, but this isn't reflected in the determination of ADI levels for additives with proven carcinogenic potential.

Additives are only tested for major physical changes, they aren't tested for neurological impacts and their effects on learning and behaviour. In the 1970s Dr Feingold wrote *"the time honoured idea that synthetic additives can be judged simply from routine carcinogenic and mutagenic standards is out of date and dangerous ... "*. Well it's even more out of date now and getting more dangerous as time marches on and nothing changes.

Similarly, additives are only tested in isolation. They are not routinely tested in any combination with other additives, which is obviously how they are consumed in real life. There is no knowledge about how these additives react with each other or the long-term cumulative effect of these innumerable combinations in our system.

It is very easy for the average Australian eating a normal healthy balanced diet to consume a combination of more than 100 different additives every day, If you find this hard to believe have a look at *Chapter 12.2 Additive consumption comparison* on page 92, and ask yourself how many different additives are you and your family eating everyday?

What little independent research into the combination effects of additives that has been done is extremely alarming. In December 2005, results published from a study conducted by the University of Liverpool into the combination effect of 4 common additives set some serious alarm bells ringing. The researchers of this study examined the toxic effect on nerve cells using a combination of four common additives – aspartame, brilliant blue, msg and quinoline yellow. They discovered that the damage each additive caused was significantly greater when the additives were eaten in combination – which of course is exactly how they are eaten in real life!

The study used additives in concentrations that theoretically reflected the amount of additives which would enter the bloodstream after a typical children's snack, and they found that the additives *stopped the nerve cells growing and interfered with the proper signalling systems.* What is so worrying about this study is that the type of foods these additives are found in, and the amounts they are talking about, is what would be in a typical snack such as a choc milk and rice crackers, or a cordial and chips.

Thankfully, however, with research such as this emerging, there is a burgeoning awareness within the scientific and medical communities that demonstrable links between diet and medical health can be identified and that these links must be investigated. In 2004, the Telethon Institute for Child Health Research in Perth, WA, instigated a study into the relationship between junk-food diets and depression. The research has been motivated by the worrying five-fold increase in depression among Australia's young people in recent years.

Astoundingly, though, there's currently no facility through FSANZ or any other government body for consumers to report or complain about adverse health effects they experience with food additives. FSANZ acknowledges that adverse reactions do occur in a small percentage of the population and recommends that such people avoid problem additives by reading labels. They don't see it as their role though to collect any information about adverse health effects.

What is so incredible about this complete lack of interest from FSANZ, is that there *is* such a mechanism for the reporting of adverse effects of agricultural and veterinary chemicals through the *Australian Pesticides and Veterinary Medicines Authority.* It would seem that our authorities are more interested in the health of the nation's livestock than its people.

Finally, food additives are tested on animals, not humans, and the relevance of animal results will be debated depending upon which side of the fence you sit. History has shown though, that many additives have passed laboratory tests and been approved for human consumption, but have afterwards been banned as more research and the actual effect on humans came to light.

The following quote sums up exactly why we should be adopting the precautionary approach when it comes to the safety of our food:

What we know:

- Every known human carcinogen causes cancer in animals.

- Every chemical known to cause brain damage in humans causes damage to the brain and nervous systems of animals.

- Every chemical known to interfere with reproductive function in humans interferes with reproductive function in animals.

- Almost every known cause of birth defects in humans also causes defects in animals.

- And, with few exceptions, when toxic chemicals harm animals, they almost always cause similar harm in humans.

**Centre for Childrens' Health and the Environment
Mount Sinai School of Medicine**

Chapter 7: Understanding labels

7.1 Introduction

Now that we know that there are many suspect additives permitted legally in our food, at least we can read the labels and choose to avoid them if we want to. Right?

Wrong.

The labels don't always tell the full story. There are several loopholes in our labelling system that can frustrate the attempts of the most dedicated consumer to make informed choices about what they eat.

FSANZ recently implemented new food-labelling legislation that came into effect in December 2002. These changes to the labelling laws improved the system in some regards by giving more information to the consumer at a glance. The nutritional-information panel was improved, and some changes were made in relation to manufacturers' requirements to detail ingredients.

The changes still did not go far enough, however, and there remain numerous inadequacies with the current laws. These loopholes exist because of industry pressure, are driven by profit, and they hinder consumers' rights to full knowledge about what is in the food we eat.

7.2 Numbers or names?

Manufacturers now have the choice of listing additives by either their number or their name. This means consumers have to be familiar with *both* the numbers and names to be able to decipher labels. It would have been a simple matter to legislate that manufacturers list both on their labels, but the manufacturers won out on this one. Manufacturers like to have the choice of which one to use as market research shows that consumers can be put off by too many chemical names.

For example, preservative 385 may be less confronting on your tinned crab meat than *calcium disodium ethylenediaminetetracetate*, and flavour enhancer 635 sounds a lot more appetising in your packet soup than *disodium 5 ribonucleotides*.

7.3   The 5% loophole

With the recent changes in the labelling laws, FSANZ had the opportunity to bring in legislation to oblige manufacturers to list *all* the ingredients in their products, no matter how small the quantity, but they didn't. Once again, the pressure from the food manufacturers won out over the rights and protection of consumers' interest.

Under the laws at the moment there's what is known as *the 5% loophole*. This gaping hole in the legislation means that manufacturers can get away with not listing additives if they are present in an ingredient that comprises *5% or less of the product*.

Antioxidants in vegetable oil are the most common example of this that I have found. Many products have vegetable oil as an ingredient, and the oil will also contain antioxidants. Some of these antioxidants (such as 310, 319 or 320) are associated with adverse health impacts, but these antioxidants aren't listed if the amount of vegetable oil in the product is less than 5% of its weight.

Often, suspect additives aren't declared on labels under the protection of this loophole. Manufacturers can list compound ingredients such as margarine and breadcrumbs, and not list what is in *those* ingredients if they make up less than 5% of the final product. These ingredients often contain suspect antioxidants, colours and preservatives, but this will not be declared on the label.

Prior to December 2002, the 5% loophole was the 10% loophole. Why FSANZ bothered to change the law from 10% to 5%, rather than just get rid of the loophole altogether, is incomprehensible from a consumer's point of view.

You can find out more about what the labels won't tell you in *Chapter 8: Labelling licence: what you need to know* on page 30.

7.4 No warnings

Despite the well-recognised adverse effect of some additives on health, FSANZ don't entertain the notion of warnings on foods. Many preservatives, especially the sulphites and nitrites, are well known to be associated with asthma attacks, and yet these are added widely to fresh and processed foods with no warnings. These preservatives are sometimes added to fresh meat, especially mince and sausages, and even to fresh fish, but the consumer has no entitlement to a warning under the current laws.

There are also many additives that are *specifically banned in foods intended for infants and young children* because of their proven adverse health impacts. This, in effect, just keeps them out of infant formula and baby food, yet FSANZ is quite happy for these same additives to be widely used in foods developed and marketed fairly and squarely at older children. For some reason it's deemed perfectly safe to feed these additives to children *over* one, yet they are prohibited and considered dangerous in foods for children *under* one. A warning on these foods that they contained additives not recommended for consumption by young children would no doubt have a dramatic effect on the sales of such foods. These include some two-minute-noodle snacks, chips, rice crackers, most sausages, frankfurts and savoury biscuits.

Despite introducing much stricter nutritional labelling, FSANZ still resists any move towards labelling of suspected carcinogenic additives in food. (After all, if it's approved, it's safe according to FSANZ.) Food labels tell us how much salt, sugar, fat and carbohydrates are in 100 grams of every product, but they don't mention the presence of potential carcinogens. If warnings declaring the presence of any known or suspected carcinogenic additives were mandatory, I am sure that consumers would vote loudly with their shopping dollars and avoid these products in droves.

Chapter 8: Labelling licence: what you need to know

8.1 Reading ingredient labels

There isn't too much to understand when it to comes to reading ingredient labels. It's more important to know how to read between the lines and recognise what's *not* on the label.

Under current laws, manufacturers must list the ingredients on all packaged foods, except if it's made and packaged on the premises (such as bread from a bakery), or if it's packaged in the presence of the customer (such as meat or cheese from a delicatessen or take-away food shop).

When reading ingredient labels, the ingredients are listed in decreasing weight, so the first ingredient listed is the largest component in the food. Additives must be listed by name or number, and by the purpose they perform in the product.

The following is an example of a label for a vegetable extract sandwich spread:

Ingredients: Hydrolysed Vegetable Protein, Sugar, Yeast Extract, Water, Salt, Colour (Caramel 150c), Wheaten Cornflour, Glucose, Spices, Emulsifier (Glycerol Monostearate), Food Acid (Citric), Vitamins, Vegetable Gum (Carrageenan), Herb and Spice Extracts

From reading this label we can learn that the main ingredient is *hydrolysed vegetable protein*. This is a less concentrated form of MSG but which is linked to the same adverse health effects as MSG.

It also contains the artificial colour *caramel 150c*. The safety of this additive is suspect and it's linked to hyperactivity, gastro-intestinal problems and kidney and liver enlargement. *Glycerol monostearate* and *citric acid* have no known adverse effects.

Carrageenan, though, is a suspected carcinogen, linked to asthma and ulcerated colitis and isn't recommended for babies and young children.

Many Australian children eat sandwich spreads with ingredients like this every day.

8.2 Hidden additives

Because of the 5% loophole, some additives aren't listed on the labels but are still present in the product. As previously mentioned, the most common example of this is antioxidants in vegetable oil. Most oils have some antioxidants in them. Many products now contain the safer ones 306–309, but many still use 310, 319 and 320, which are some of the worst additives linked to cancer and serious adverse health effects.

If you don't want to eat these chemicals, unfortunately the only way you can know for sure what's in these products, is to ring the company and ask what's in the oil they use.

Be on the look out for antioxidants in any products with ingredient lists that include fats such as animal oil, animal fat, butter, fat, copha, lard, milk solids, palm oil, shortening, tallow, vegetable oil, margarine. Common product lines found to contain antioxidants in oil, but not listed on the label, include biscuits, bread, spreads, soy milk drinks, cooking sauces, ice cream cones, baby food, tinned fish and frozen products such as pastries, pies, fish fingers, chicken nuggets, frozen desserts, potato products and ready meals.

8.3 No-MSG claims

Due to the bad press MSG has suffered in relation to widespread adverse health effects, many manufacturers emblazon "No MSG" messages on their packaging to attract the health conscious shopper.

Be Wary. Many, many products carrying these claims are very misleading.

Often they don't contain MSG in the form of food additive 621, but they will contain other flavour enhancers (620–635) that are associated with the same range of adverse health impacts, but are less well known. Avoid anything with flavour enhancers or hydrolysed vegetable protein if you're wanting to avoid MSG because of its health effects.

See section *9.1: MSG and flavour enhancers* on page 37 for more information.

8.4 Natural colour

Many manufacturers like to use the word *natural* wherever possible to assist in marketing and to attract customers. *Natural colour* is a description often found on labels in relation to Cochineal (120), Caramel (150) and Annatto (160b).

- *Cochineal* is derived from crushed insects. It is linked to hyperactivity and is suspected of embryo toxicity.

- *Caramels 150(i), 150(ii), 150(iii)* and *150(iv)* have nothing at all to do with the image of browned sugar the caramel name suggests. These colours are produced synthetically by the treatment of carbohydrates in the presence of ammonia, ammonium sulphate, sulphur dioxide and/or sodium hydroxide. The safety of all these colours is suspect with *150(i)* seeming to be the safest, but more research is needed.

- *Annatto* is derived from the seed of the tropical Annatto tree. It is linked anecdotally to behaviour and learning problems, asthma, hyperactivity, urticaria and allergies.

Many food additives are derived from natural sources, but this doesn't necessarily mean that they are any safer than other additives. Be aware of this when shopping, and don't be swayed by claims of natural colours or ingredients. Natural or not, they may not be the safest choice for you.

8.5   Flavours

The use of flavours in food products isn't subject to the same laws as food additives. There are several thousand flavours permitted for use, and they don't have to be described on labels. The reason for this is that their chemical composition is too complex. A coffee flavour for example may consist of several *thousand* odorous materials, each composed of a different chemical type. This is the case for all characteristic food flavours. The bottom line is there's no way of knowing exactly what's in a flavour, so if you're concerned about additives and chemicals, it may be best to avoid all products marked *flavour added* including those labelled *nature identical flavour.*

Manufacturers do play on the perception that fruit and natural flavours are seen as healthiest by consumers, but be aware that the use of "fruit" flavours doesn't necessarily mean that there is any fruit in the product. For example, *strawberry yoghurt* must have some strawberries in it, but *strawberry flavoured yoghurt* doesn't have to contain any strawberries and may be completely artificially flavoured.

8.6   Organic claims

Consumers, in general, are becoming more discerning and health conscious. Manufacturers have picked up on this and compete for our shopping dollars with labelling that leaps out and attracts shoppers wanting healthier products. As a result, the terms *organic* and *all natural* are appearing more and more on labels across the complete product range.

Beware though: a product isn't organic unless it's labelled *certified organic*; and many *all natural* products do, on closer examination, contain many suspect additives, even if they are naturally sourced. Remember, *natural* doesn't necessarily mean safer.

8.7   No artificial preservatives

No artificial preservatives is another common phrase found on labels. It is designed to attract or sway shoppers' choice in favour of the product. This is often a true statement, but it doesn't necessarily mean the product is preservative free. There are many preservatives that are naturally sourced and, as with colours, *natural* doesn't necessarily mean safer, particularly for asthmatics.

8.8   Advertising by omission

This is another common ploy to fool the consumer. Manufacturers naturally want to advertise the best points of their products, not draw your attention to the less appealing aspects. After all, they want you to buy their product to help their profits.

For example, the packet of a popular cheese-flavoured snack is emblazoned with an attention grabbing:

> *No Preservatives*
>
> *No Artificial Colours*
>
> *No Artificial Flavours*

These statements are true. What they don't draw your attention to is the use of three flavour enhancers: MSG (621), *disodium guanylate* (627) and *disodium inosinate* (631). All of these additives are prohibited in foods for infants and young children and are linked to an array of adverse health effects ranging from headaches, asthma, sleep disturbance, behaviour and learning problems in children. Unfortunately, children would be the major consumers of products like this.

8.9   Customer enquiry services

If you have a query about what's in a product, you can contact the manufacturer whose contact details will be on the label. The bigger companies have toll-free numbers and specially trained staff, but many smaller manufacturers don't, so you may end up talking to the factory supervisor or someone with little or no knowledge about food additives.

Many of the larger brands are owned by the larger food manufacturing outfits such as Unilever, Goodman Fielder, etc so you may find many different brands serviced by the same customer-service centres. Supermarket home-brand lines are often actually manufactured by these big names also, so you might find, for example, that the contact number for *Coles Homebrand Fish Fingers* is the same as a *Birds Eye* product, and that the products are, in fact, identical.

From my experience researching this book, most of the customer-service staff I encountered were well meaning and helpful, some outstandingly so. A small number were not, and some were quite hostile and totally unhelpful when I explained that I wanted to know about additives because of health concerns.

Be aware that if you ring for more information on a product, that the staff answering your call may know very little if anything about the potential health impacts of food additives. The phone staff are *company trained* to promote products and reassure consumers that they should purchase their products, and they only have the information available that is provided for them by the company. Usually they operate from databases with product specifications that match the information on the labels, so they often know nothing more than you know from reading the label.

If you want to know more (for example, if there's any antioxidant in a vegetable oil which was not listed on the label), you may initially be told quite definitely that if it's not on the label, it's not in the product. Many of these staff aren't aware of the 5% loophole and will swear black and blue that their labels are accurate, only to be forced to go away and check and find out they were wrong.

Don't be afraid to insist politely that you really need to know for health reasons. Ask them to check with their suppliers, if necessary, to give you a 100% correct answer.

It is your right as a consumer to be able to find out exactly what is in the food you eat. Don't be intimidated or put off with inadequate answers and try to have the confidence to complain to a supervisor if your enquiry isn't answered adequately.

The only way consumers are going to influence manufacturers is by letting them know what we will and won't buy. If you do find out that a product has an additive you wish to avoid, make sure you tell the company representative that you'll avoid their product because of their use of unsafe additives. This type of feedback, as well as actually voting with our shopping dollars and *not* buying the products, is the only way to make the manufacturers sit up and take note.

Chapter 9: The ones to watch out for

Although a full list of all additives and their potential health effects is provided at the back of this book for your reference, the widespread and increasing use of some additives is so disturbing that they require special mention in this chapter. This way, you, the consumer, have all the necessary information to decide which additives you wish to avoid.

9.1 MSG and flavour enhancers

MSG is the sodium salt of glutamic acid. In its processed form as the food additive MSG 621, it is a white powder which looks like salt or sugar. It has no taste of its own and no nutritional value, but is used to enhance or modify flavours of foods. Most people have heard of it due to its widespread use in Chinese food and the resulting bad press of what became known as "Chinese restaurant syndrome". After eating Chinese food, some people were reporting a wide range of adverse health effects including sweating, heart palpitations, sleeplessness, heartburn, asthma, rashes, nausea and migraines. Studies have shown that while just 0.5 milligrams of MSG is enough to cause symptoms in sensitive people, some Chinese meals were found to contain up to 10 milligrams of MSG.

Discovered in Japan, MSG was not commonly added to western diets until after World War II when American food manufacturers began adding it to their products. No significant safety studies were performed and, since the 1940s, MSG usage has doubled every decade. This represents one of the most significant changes to our diets in the past 50 years.

Originally, there were no restrictions on the use of MSG in foods, but in 1969 it was prohibited from use in baby foods in America due to damning research demonstrating that MSG caused detrimental effects on young animals, particularly the brain and nervous systems. Pregnant monkeys fed MSG gave birth to brain-damaged offspring, and this was also found with pregnant rats.

MSG is still prohibited from use in baby foods in Australia, because of its proven ability to damage the brain and developing nervous system, but this effectively only keeps it out of infant formulas and baby food. MSG is still widely used in many foods eaten regularly by young children and pregnant women, with no warnings required on the labels.

MSG stands for *Monosodium Glutamate*, and it is the adverse effect of excess glutamate which is of concern. It is very important to understand the difference between *natural glutamate* such as that found in broccoli and cheese, and *processed free glutamate* as is found in the food additive MSG, because the glutamate industry goes to great lengths and expense to reassure consumers that MSG is safe and beneficial, when in fact there is a huge difference between the effects of natural and processed glutamate.

Glutamate is an important neurotransmitter and, in normal levels in the body, it does an important job allowing the cells in the brain to communicate with each other. However, when the brain is exposed to excessive amounts of glutamate, serious damage can occur. Glutamate belongs to a group of amino acids (including cysteine, aspartate and glutamate) which are classified as *"excitotoxins"*. Excitotoxins are substances that, when applied to neurons (brain cells) will cause them to become overstimulated and, if overstimulated too much, will die. Put simply, they kill our brain cells. Although this effect is a worry for anyone, it is most concerning in relation to children and pregnant women.

Low levels of glutamate in the form of MSG are found naturally in many foods such as tomatoes, broccoli, mushrooms, spinach and grapes. Unless you're truly allergic or intolerant to MSG, eating MSG at these natural levels is not a problem. In this state, the glutamate is bound to protein and is present in low concentrations, so that when we eat these foods, they are digested slowly and the glutamate is released into our bloodstream at the right concentration. The glutamate is then taken up into the brain at the right levels where it helps to perform essential functions within our bodies. Natural levels of bound glutamate like this in natural foods are not something you need to be concerned about.

However, this has got very little to do with the high levels of processed free glutamate, which is what the food additive MSG is made up of. To make the food additive MSG, the food manufacturers extract the natural glutamate from the raw ingredients, and the glutamate is processed so that it is no longer bound to protein. It is now called *processed free glutamate* – and it is highly, highly concentrated at levels that far exceed the levels found naturally in foods. When we eat artificially high doses of MSG like this, such as is found in our chips and snack foods, it is like a shot or a dose of free glutamate into our bloodstream. We end up with excessive quantities of glutamate in our system, and this is a problem.

The blood–brain barrier is a system in the walls of the capillaries within the brain that works to keep toxic substances, including excess glutamate levels, from entering the brain. However, there are parts of the brain that aren't protected by this barrier. This allows excess glutamates to enter the brain. It is also known that prolonged, high levels of excessive glutamate exposure can cause glutamates to seep through the blood–brain barrier and impact the brain.

In natural foods containing glutamate, the different amino acids compete with each other to get into the brain, so only a little of each gets in at the right concentrations. By contrast when we eat foods high in processed free glutamate, excess glutamate on its own gets in at much higher concentrations than normal, causing excitotoxic effects of the brain.

Young children are particularly at risk because the blood brain barrier is not fully developed during infancy and childhood. This allows excess glutamate to be delivered to the brain. Damage is also known to occur *in utero* as MSG has been shown to cross the placenta and concentrate in the foetus at levels twice that of the mother. It is this neurotoxic action of glutamate on the brain that is the most concerning adverse health effect linked to MSG. The effect on young children is again most worrisome because of the disproportionate dose they receive after eating foods containing extremely high levels of MSG.

Ongoing research has implicated excess glutamate as a contributing factor in learning disorders, brain tumours, hyperactivity, Parkinson's disease, Alzheimer's disease and endocrine-system problems developing later in life. MSG is also linked to asthma and a wide range of serious adverse health effects including sleep disturbances, migraine, irritability and depression.

Most recently, MSG is being implicated in the alarming obesity epidemic confronting developed countries all over the world. Research conducted in 2005 by a team of Spanish and German scientists found that when given to rats at concentrations only slightly higher than those found in human foods, MSG caused a massive 40% increase in appetite. MSG is used in foods as a flavour enhancer to make foods taste better, so it is not surprising that its use in foods leads to such dramatic overeating. Many are now linking the steadily increasing use of MSG in our foods since the 1950's to the parallel increase in obesity rates within western society. What is more concerning though is that these findings are nothing new. Studies done as far back as 1968 first identified that MSG induced obesity in animal studies.

Because the damaging effect of MSG on the developing brain is so well documented, many researchers are now wondering if this exponential increase in MSG consumption is also a major contributing factor to the increased levels of depression, violence, behavioural and learning disorders evident in western societies around the world today. In January 2005 British researchers reported that changes in diet over the past fifty years appear to be an important factor behind a significant rise in mental ill health. Research has also confirmed that MSG has an alarming effect on anger. Studies done as far back as 1979 revealed that MSG exposure was able to produce intense rage reactions in animal subjects.

With so much evidence confirming that MSG is able to produce such serious detrimental effects, it is of great concern that the use of this food additive is becoming so wide spread that it is becoming very difficult to avoid it without a concerted effort. This generation of children are eating worrying amounts of MSG and their exposure is beginning before they are born via their mothers' diet. What is of even more concern is the knowledge that humans are the most susceptible to physical damage from ingested MSG. According to Professor Russell Blaylock, author of *Health and Nutrition Secrets That Can Save your Life*, humans possess a sensitivity to MSG five times greater than that of the mouse and twenty times greater than the rhesus monkey.

The evidence is clear that MSG causes damage to animals. Why on earth are we continuing to consume this toxin in our foods?

9.2 Avoiding MSG isn't as easy as it should be

In response to the growing concern and awareness about the adverse effects of MSG, food manufacturers and the glutamate manufacturers have joined together to form a special lobby group called *The Glutamate Association* to counter any negative claims about MSG. This group has an obvious vested interest in keeping MSG and other flavour enhancers on the market and in keeping information off food labels.

As we have seen, manufacturers can list additives either by name or by a number and the function they perform. MSG is often not on the label, but is instead identified as *flavour enhancer 621*, which isn't so readily recognisable. Alternatively, and increasingly common, they use other glutamates and flavour enhancers such as 620, 622, 623, 624, 625, 627, 631 and 635. These aren't as well known to consumers. These other glutamates are all linked to the same adverse health impacts as MSG, while 627, 631 and 635 are known to cause other serious adverse health effects.

The use in particular of flavour enhancer 635 (*disodium 5 ribonucleotides*) has only been permitted in Australian foods for the past five years, yet it is making its presence known loudly. It has been linked with a wide range of adverse effects including sleep disturbance, skin complaints and the appearance of a distinctive, unbearably itchy rash known as *ribo rash*. The adverse effects of this additive are becoming so common that the Royal Prince Alfred Hospital Allergy Unit commissioned a clinical study in 2003 to investigate the complaints.

Concern about the use of MSG and other similar additives is a global issue. In June 2003 it was reported that the Education Ministry in Thailand banned the use of MSG in school canteen meals along with other harmful additives. If officials in Thailand are sufficiently concerned about the health impacts of these additives, it begs the question why aren't regulators here in Australia?

9.3 Ways to disguise MSG in foods.

Today, hundreds of thousands of tonnes of MSG are produced and added to foods that we eat. An additive that used to be found mainly in Chinese and very spicy foods and was eaten infrequently is now so widespread it's getting difficult to avoid.

It is found in most snacks and savoury biscuits, sauces and condiments, preserved and "fresh meats" (including bacon, polony, ham and sausages), many tinned savoury foods, packet soups, frozen meals and packaged meals, and even in some margarines.

As consumers are becoming more wary of MSG, manufacturers are cleverly using other non-regulated ingredients that also contain high levels of processed free glutamate, but which are not pure MSG, to avoid having to list MSG on their labels. These ingredients allow manufacturers to still get the MSG effect on the flavour of their product, but these ingredients are still high in the excitotoxic processed free glutamate.

One of the most common ingredients used as a substitute for MSG is *Hydrolysed Vegetable Protein*. This healthy sounding ingredient is commonly found in many products which quite legally promote themselves as being MSG free. What the labels will neglect to mention is the fact that the product is loaded with another form of highly concentrated processed free glutamate, which you now know to have the same adverse effects as MSG.

In his book *Excitotoxins: The Taste That Kills*, Dr Russell Blaylock (a Professor of Neurosurgery at the Medical University of Mississippi), lists the following common sources of concentrated processed free glutamate (MSG) which are often included in foods but not labelled as MSG:

Additives that always contain MSG

monosodium glutamate
hydrolysed vegetable protein **
hydrolysed plant protein
plant protein extract
calcium caseinate
hydrolysed oat flour
hydrolysed (anything else)

potassium glutamate
hydrolysed protein
autolysed yeast
sodium caseinate
yeast extract
textured protein

Additives that frequently contain processed free glutamate (MSG)

malt extract
bouillon
stock
natural flavouring
natural beef or chicken flavour

malt flavour
broth
flavouring
spices
seasoning

Dr Blaycock provides this explanation of what exactly this healthy sounding ingredient really is.

Hydrolysed vegetable protein

Hydrolysed vegetable protein is a concentrated form of natural MSG that is now often used by manufacturers instead of MSG as a way around consumer concern. Often, products with high amounts of HVP boldly market themselves as "MSG free" to attract consumers who are unaware that HVP contains high concentrations of glutamates and has the same health effects as MSG.

HVP is made from junk vegetables selected for their high quantity of excitotoxins; e.g. glutamate. The vegetables are boiled in a vat of sulphuric acid for several hours then the acid is neutralised with caustic soda. The brown sludge is scraped off the top and dried into a powder. The powder contains known carcinogens and dicarboxylic acid, the safety of which is unknown. MSG is often added to this powder. Finally, the powder is put in our food, including baby food, and we eat it.

So, avoiding MSG isn't always that easy. Luckily most people aren't truly allergic to MSG. If you are, though, you'll need to avoid all products that have any of the above ingredients.

If you want to avoid MSG because of the concerning adverse effects, you'll need to decide how far you want to take it. It can be very limiting to avoid all food with *flavour* or *seasoning* as an ingredient, but the facts are that there is no way of knowing exactly what is in these ingredients.

Depending on your health and motivation, you may just choose to avoid the main sources and not buy anything with flavour enhancers 620–637 or hydrolysed vegetable protein on the label. By adopting a simple change like this, you'll be making a very significant improvement to your overall health and wellbeing.

9.4 Aspartame and artificial sweeteners

Aspartame is another food additive that is becoming increasingly commonplace in the foods we buy. It is also associated with a concerning array of adverse health effects. Most people assume that Aspartame and artificial sweeteners are only used in diet foods and drinks and, as such, many of us aren't aware that we're consuming these additives.

Like MSG, the use of Aspartame has escalated rapidly, and it is now finding its way into an alarming array of mainstream foods. The worst examples that I found of this were Aspartame in sausages and rice crackers. It is also now found commonly in yoghurts, snacks, desserts, mints, cordials, juices, instant coffee drinks, vitamins and medicines.

Aspartame was first approved for use in 1981, and controversy has simmered since then about the safety of the additive and the circumstances surrounding its approval in the US. Scientists fiercely debated the safety of Aspartame for 20 years prior to its approval. Despite significant scientific data showing a link to the development of brain tumours in rats, the manufacturers, Searle Laboratory, kept pushing for its approval.

One month after approving the additive for use, US Food and Drug Administration Commissioner Arthur Hull Hayes, resigned from his post and became a senior consultant for the public-relations firm that managed Searle's account for Aspartame.

Aspartame is considered by some to be the most dangerous substance on the market that is added to foods. It accounts for over 75% of the adverse reactions reported to the US Food and Drug Administration, yet the additive is still widely permitted and no warning labelling is required.

The range of symptoms and ailments attributed to Aspartame in a 1994 Department of Health and Human Services report include:

Headache, migraines, dizziness, seizures, numbness, rashes, depression, fatigue, irritability, tachycardia, insomnia, vision problems, hearing loss, heart palpitations, breathing difficulties, slurred speech, tinnitus, vertigo, memory loss and joint pain.

Aspartame is an excitotoxin, as is MSG. Excessive exposure to Aspartame can cause damage to the brain cells and, as with MSG, children and infants (including foetuses) are most at risk because of the undeveloped blood–brain barrier. *For this reason pregnant women should avoid Aspartame, and it should not be given to children at all.*

Aspartame is a compound made up of 50% phenylalanine. Phenylalanine is an amino acid normally found in the brain. People with the genetic disorder called phenylketonuria (PKU) cannot metabolise phenylalanine, and over-exposure can lead to serious complications, even death. For this reason, it's recommended that people with PKU don't consume Aspartame and a warning to this effect is often carried by products, such as diet drinks, containing Aspartame.

However, even people who don't have PKU can develop excessive levels of phenylalanine in the brain after excessive consumption of Aspartame. Excess phenylalanine can cause the levels of serotonin in the brain to decrease, which may lead to emotional disorders such as depression.

Anecdotal evidence exists of people drinking six to eight cans of diet drink daily and experiencing a range of adverse symptoms including mood swings, rages, depression and headaches. These dramatically improved or vanished when Aspartame was removed from their diets.

Aspartame is also linked to brain cancer. It has been shown experimentally to cause brain tumours in rats. In fact, a two-year study by the manufacturer even confirmed this result, yet it was still approved for use!

More recently, scientists from the Ramizzini Institute for Cancer Research in Italy published alarming results from a comprehensive study completed in 2005. This study confirmed that Aspartame caused lymphomas and leukaemia in female animals fed Aspartame *in doses very close to the acceptable daily intake set for humans*. Some of the animals in this study also developed brain tumours.

Despite this study there is no move by FSANZ to review or limit the use of Aspartame in Australian foods and, in fact, the use of Aspartame is becoming more and more widespread. It is estimated now that 1 in every 15 people are regular consumers of Aspartame, and many of these are children. As we face a future with half of all Australian kids overweight or obese, more parents are likely to choose "diet" products for their children, and this proportion is going to rise. It is very concerning to think about what the long term effect of regular Aspartame consumption might be in this generation of kids.

It is interesting to note that the incidence of brain cancer in the US, Australia and many other countries has increased substantially since 1981. This coincides with the introduction of Aspartame. It also coincides with the advent of mobile phones and, no doubt, many other coincidences. Still, many researchers aren't surprised at this statistic, given the proven ability of Aspartame to cause brain tumours in animals.

9.5 Other artificial sweeteners

The most common artificial sweeteners in Australia are Aspartame, Saccharin, Acesulphame Potassium, Sucralose and Cyclamates, but they may appear on product labels as more appealing sounding brand names such as Nutrasweet, Equal, Splenda or Sweet and Low.

- Saccharin is known to cause cancer in lab animals and is classified as a weak human carcinogen.

- Acesulphame Potassium likewise has been shown to promote tumour growth in laboratory animals, and a large question mark hangs over the safety of its long-term use in humans.

- Sucralose has been recently added to the Australian Food Standards. There is abundant concern about the safety of this sweetener, and a need for more investigation into its long term use and its effects in humans.

- Cyclamates are regarded as potential carcinogens and have been banned previously in the US and UK, but are still allowed in Australia. However, in May 2004, FSANZ released results of a survey that found that many Australians are exceeding the maximum daily intake of this additive. As a result, FSANZ are to consider changing the relevant standard to reduce the permissible levels of cyclamates in Australian foods.

With the growing consumer concern and aversion to taking many of the more common artificial sweeteners, a new breed of "natural" artificial sweeteners has emerged in our food supply. These additives are known as *polyols* and include Sorbitol 420, Mannitol 421, Isomalt 953, Maltitol 965, Lactitol 966, Xylitol 967, Erythritol 968 and Polydextrose 1200.

As with many of the newer additives, there is conflicting information and doubt about the long term safety of these substances. All of these sugar free sweeteners are known to cause gastric upsets and diarrhoea in large doses, and many consumers have reported these symptoms as an adverse side effect of even moderate consumption. *Xylitol* is widely used and promoted as a good choice for diabetics in particular, but some caution is advised as earlier studies did cite a link to cancer. More recent studies have countered these findings, but it may well be sensible to avoid consuming these substances on a regular basis.

9.6   Nitrates and nitrites

Sodium nitrate (250) and sodium nitrite (251) are salt-like chemicals found commonly in processed and cured meats including ham, polony, bacon and frankfurters. They are added to preserve the meats and to add colour and flavour. Their role as a preservative is important as it's the presence of nitrates or nitrites that prevents the bacteria that causes botulism. However, these additives are *widely considered to be toxic and carcinogenic in humans.*

Nitrites are capable of entering the bloodstream and changing the nature of the red blood cells responsible for oxygen transport. When the blood's ability to carry oxygen is impaired, this can lead to a condition known as *methemoglobinemia*, which can result in dizziness, laboured breathing and even death from asphyxiation if nitrite exposure is prolonged. Infants are especially more susceptible to this condition and as such *nitrites aren't permitted in foods intended for infants and young children.*

Nitrites and nitrates are known to react with substances in meats called amines to form *nitrosamines,* which are hazardous poisons and definite animal carcinogens. The question whether humans suffer from cancer due to exposure to these compounds hasn't yet been answered. Studies showing that nitrosamines initiate a wide range of cancers in various animal species strongly suggest, though, that they are carcinogenic in humans also.

Studies have also shown that the effect of nitrosamines can be inhibited by the action of antioxidants such as vitamins C and E. It is recommended that if you eat products with nitrates and nitrites, eat them with antioxidants (e.g. a glass of orange juice or a tomato salad) to minimise the potential harmful effects of the nitrosamines formed.

As with all of these suspect additives, there's varied scientific data on both sides. With this particular group, it's very likely that they can cause cancer in humans. Once again, dose for weight, children are more susceptible.

Some researchers are more definite about a link between these foods and cancer, especially in children. In his book *Unreasonable Risk*, Dr Samuel Epstein, Chairman of the Cancer Prevention Coalition, provides this excerpt from the Dirty Dozen, a 1995 survey of carcinogens in 12 common consumer products:

Beef frankfurters

Children eating up to about a dozen each month are at an approximately four-fold increased risk of brain cancer and seven-fold increased risk of leukaemia. (This is due to the formation of a nitrosamine carcinogen, by the interaction of nitrate and natural amines in meat.)

Effectively, FSANZ restriction on these additives only prevents manufacturers from putting them in baby foods. What about all the polony, frankfurts and processed meats that most Australian children eat regularly from the age of one and up? Surely, if there's enough evidence of concern to warrant these substances being banned in infants' food, there should be some sort of warning on the labels of other foods containing these substances, so parents can make informed choices about whether or not they want to feed these chemicals to their kids.

Because of the strong likelihood that these substances will prove to be human carcinogens also, it's advisable for everyone, especially children, to avoid excess consumption of foods containing nitrites and nitrates. Parents can limit children's consumption of obvious sources such as polony and ham and substitute other safer alternatives such as cold roast meats and preservative-free sausages. These are usually readily available through butchers and health food shops.

9.7   Artificial colours

Many people are aware of the link between well-known artificial colours and hyperactivity, but far fewer people are aware that many colours widely used in our foods today are proven or suspected carcinogens. As with MSG and Aspartame, the use of colours in our foods seems to be growing all the time, and artificial colours are now found in an amazing array of foods that we eat every day.

Many people who try to avoid the most vibrant artificial colours would be shocked to find out how many colours they are unwittingly consuming every day in seemingly natural, uncoloured foods. Some chocolate biscuits are a good example. Most of us would assume that biscuits such as Tim Tams are made chocolate by the use of cocoa, but in fact that lovely chocolate coating is a mixture of Tartrazine (102), Sunset Yellow (110), Allura Red (129), Brilliant Blue (133), and Caramel (150).

Similarly, many cheese slices these days contain Annatto (160b), Curcumin (100) and Titanium dioxide (171). Fruit juices and juice drinks are another common source of a daily dose of artificial colours including Caramel (150), which is found in many apple drinks, and Sunset Yellow (110) and Tartrazine (102), which are found in many orange-flavoured drinks.

It is this widespread use of colours in our foods that is concerning, especially when the use of colours is purely a manufacturing ploy to enhance the appeal of a product to consumers. Colours in food perform no function other than cosmetic. They are there just to make the food look better to the consumer.

It can be argued that in many cases the colours are used to fool the consumer by making inferior products look more enticing and real. Whatever the reasons, we're now consuming more of these substances in our diets than ever before. Their use is so widespread in processed foods that, in the US, it's estimated that the average daily consumption of artificial colours ranges from *15 to 50 milligrams per person per day*. We can assume that Australian dietary trends would reflect this level of consumption also.

Once again, this is most concerning in relation to children, as it's in children's foods that we see the most obvious and heaviest overuse of artificial colours. The insidious appearance of colours in staple foods such as fruit juice, cheese, margarines and biscuits is alarming, especially when parents trying to limit consumption of colours by their families, may well be unaware that these basic food items contain a wide range of colouring additives.

The health concerns associated with colours are varied. The most well known effect is hyperactivity. This applies mainly to a range of colours known as the Coal Tar and AZO dyes. These include 102, 104, 110, 122, 123, 124, 132, 133, 142, 151 and 155. Over the past 20 years, more than a dozen of these types of additives have been taken off the market following laboratory confirmation that they were toxic or carcinogenic. Many of these additives have not been reviewed in relation to safety for 30 years or more, and, for many, the original safety testing was minimal and inconclusive. In 2007, the European Food Standards Agency initiated a systematic review of some colour additives due to mounting concern over their long term safety and lack of accurate safety data. While this process will take many years to complete, the first additive reviewed under this project, colour Red 2G, was found to be likely carcinogenic and immediately recalled from use.

Abundant concern also exists surrounding the effect of these additives on children, particularly adverse behaviour and learning impacts. A 2003 study published by the respected *Archives of Disease in Childhood,* found that some colour additives can have an adverse effect on all children, not just those prone to hyperactivity or allergies. The results of this study were confirmed in September 2007 in a repeat study commissioned by the UK Food Standards Agency and conducted by the University of Southhampton. The results of the most recent study were published in *The Lancet* and clearly confirmed the wealth of anecdotal experience linking colours and preservatives to adverse behaviour effects in children.

The research was conducted using 3 year olds and 8 – 9 year olds, and, importantly, the findings confirmed again that the additives caused adverse effects within the *general population* and not just those kids with a history of hyperactivity or ADHD. The "significantly adverse effects" observed included tantrums, poor concentration and slow progress at school.

The additives tested in the study were colours Sunset Yellow (110), Tartrazine (102), Carmoisine (122), Ponceau 4R (124), Quinoline Yellow (104), Allura Red (129) and preservative Sodium Benzoate (211). Combinations of these additives are commonly found in childrens' products such as cordials, fruit juices, museli bars, yoghurts, fruit sticks, milk drinks as well as confectionary and soft drink.

In the wake of these findings, consumer groups worldwide called for regulatory agencies to act on the evidence that the additives could cause harm to children, and called for a ban to be imposed on the use of these additives or, at the very least, a clear warning issued to parents to avoid such products. Incredibly though, the official response has been far from adequate. In the UK, the FSA has referred the findings to the European FSA for evaluation, a process which could take years. Here in Australia, FSANZ have taken NO official action, aside from issuing a statement that parents of hyperactive children may wish to avoid these additives, a response which completely misses the central finding of the study, that these additives have now been shown to be of concern for all children.

Several colours still permitted in Australia are *banned* in other countries because of their proven links to cancer. These colours include Amaranth (123), Food Green (142), Brilliant Black (151), Carbon Black (153) and Brown HT (155). There are many other colours permitted in Australia that are strongly suspected of being carcinogenic based on animal tests, but are still widely used, mainly in children's foods, with no warnings required on the labels.

Other "natural" colour additives such as Annatto (160b) are believed to be associated with behaviour and learning impairment, especially in children. This additive is becoming more and more widespread and is commonly found in foods that are coloured white, cream or yellow including cheese and margarine.

Although Annatto is regarded as safe in Australia, it's interesting to note that as of June 2003, the toxicity of this additive was still being evaluated and considered by the *World Health Organisation Joint Expert Committee on Food Additives (JECFA)*.

Similarly, JECFA has also requested more information about a reproductive toxicity study into Curcumin (100), as this colour is suspected of causing animal genetic damage and posing a risk to conception. Although safety studies are still continuing worldwide, these additives are allowed to be widely used in our foods with no warnings required.

Tartrazine (102) is another insidious colour that is now found in many foods including juices. It is linked to a wide array of health problems including irritability, gastric upsets and sleep disturbances. Breastfeeding mothers have found that eliminating this additive has helped their "colicky" babies sleep better and be less fretful. It is also known to disrupt the body's metabolism of zinc and is implicated as a contributing factor in ADD and ADHD in some children.

One of the main problems in relation to determining the safety or otherwise of these substances lies in the initial testing. Prior to introduction, additives are tested for acute toxicity, but even if laboratory tests show links to cancer or other serious side effects, this doesn't necessarily mean that they will be prohibited. As we have seen, despite clear evidence in animal tests that a substance does cause damage, a lower "safe" level of consumption is determined, and often these additives go on to be included in our foods.

These additives also aren't tested for *neuropsychological* effects such as hyperactivity and subtle behaviour and learning impacts. Also, they are tested in isolation, not in combination, which is how they are actually consumed in our diets.

This is why there's so much conflicting evidence about the safety of many of these substances. As consumers, *we need to remember that just because these additives are currently permitted in our foods, it doesn't guarantee that they are safe.*

When shopping, the best rule of thumb is to avoid any obviously coloured foods, and don't assume that plain coloured foods are necessarily colour free. White ice cream usually contains a couple of colours, and chocolate-flavoured biscuits, ice creams and drinks are often made brown by blending several of the most toxic colour additives.

Be on the look out also for subtle colours such as Caramel and Annatto. These colours are often marketed aggressively using the label *No Artificial Colours*. As we have seen, this in no way means they are actually any better or safer for us.

9.8 Preservatives

Preservatives are a necessary addition to processed foods if we want to have access to products that will remain fresh. Once again, however, the use of preservatives is growing rapidly, and we're now finding more and more preservatives creeping into our staple foods such as bread, fruit juice, margarine and even supposedly fresh meats and fish. For this reason consumers need to be aware of the health impacts associated with the different groups of preservatives.

Unlike colours, most preservatives are generally not linked to cancer, but other serious concerns are held about the long-term cumulative effect of these additives in our diets. Some preservative groups are known to be dangerous to asthmatics, whilst others are known to contribute to behaviour and learning problems, especially in sensitive children. Unlike reactions to colours, which are often dramatic and obvious, reactions to preservatives are often delayed and subtle, and therefore difficult to identify and pinpoint.

Preservatives found to cause problems are described in the following sections.

9.9 Sulphites (220–228)

These substances have been shown to trigger asthma attacks in sufferers. The sulphur dioxide gas (a major irritant to asthmatics) contained in sulphites is released and inhaled when the food is swallowed. Anyone susceptible to asthma should avoid foods containing sulphites. Be aware also that fresh fish, seafood and mince may have sodium metabisulphite sprinkled on it to keep it looking fresh. This is an odourless white powder which you cannot see on the produce, so, if in doubt, check.

These additives are also of wider concern as 220 is a suspected mutagen and possible teratogen and is linked to a variety of ill effects including gastric irritation and liver toxicity. Other sulphites (221–228) are linked widely to gastric irritation, nausea, diarrhoea and rashes, so many people, not just asthmatics, may wish to avoid these additives where possible.

In August 2005 FSANZ released the results from their 21st Total Diet Study into the consumption of sulphites, benzoates and sorbates. This study revealed that a significant proportion of the population takes in more than the Acceptable Daily Intake (ADI) of sulphites and benzoates, particularly for children ages 2-5 years who, according to the report, may be taking in up to four times the sulphite ADI. Since these figures are based on food consumption in 1995, well before the explosion of dried fruit based snacks for kids, it is extremely likely that these findings seriously underestimate actual consumption, especially by children.

9.10 Proprionates (280–283)

These preservatives were once not very common in Australian foods, but they are now contained in most supermarket bread and bread products and many bakery products. The use of these additives is so widespread in bread products in Australia that it's hard to find products that don't use them. They are now appearing in other healthy foods such as fruit juices, cheese and dried fruit.

Proprionates are associated with an array of adverse health problems including behaviour and learning problems, lethargy, gastro-intestinal problems, migraines, irritability, depression, sleep disturbances and growing pains. They are also implicated in causing the same symptoms and great distress in babies who are exposed through breast milk.

Calcium proprionate (282) is appearing more and more commonly in our foods, not just in fresh bread products. All mainstream breadcrumb products contain this additive. So, to avoid it, you need to either make your own breadcrumbs or look for organic varieties. It is also in many prepared frozen foods such as some fish fingers and many products coated with or containing breadcrumbs. Many frozen sausage rolls contain bread crumbs in the mix. These will contain 282, but it will likely not be declared on the label. If an ingredient label lists breadcrumbs but the breakdown of the breadcrumbs isn't provided, you would need to ring and check to find out if 282 is in the product.

Calcium proprionate 282 is banned in the UK because it's known to cause skin rashes in bakery workers. A recent study in Darwin confirmed that consumption of this additive can adversely affect children's behaviour. The results of this study have been published in the *Journal of Paediatrics and Child Health*, August 2002, and confirm that proprionates appear to have a dramatic effect on many children in relation to behaviour, disposition and general happiness. This is one of the first additives that many families eliminate from their diets, and the positive improvements in children's behaviour is often the most noticeable flow on effect of this simple change. For some families the change can be quite startling, with many parents reporting significant improvement in children's school progress, much improved self control and anger management and the disappearance of numerous antisocial or difficult behaviours.

There is also a wealth of anecdotal evidence from mothers linking this additive to sleeping and gastrointestinal problems in young babies, with many women reporting that colicky, restless babies improved significantly when this additive is removed from the mother's diet.

9.11 Benzoates (210–213)

Benzoates are found in soft drinks and particularly cordials. They also are considered dangerous for asthmatics and people sensitive to Aspirin (salicylates). They are also linked more widely to a range of adverse effects including hyperactivity, eye and skin irritation, and gastric burning. Sodium benzoate (211) is associated with liver, kidney and neurotoxic effects and is also regarded as a possible teratogen.

Benzoates are quickly gaining a reputation as one of the worst additives in relation to provoking behaviour and learning problems in children. Research published in 2004 in the peer review journal *Archives of Disease in Childhood* confirmed that benzoate preservatives have a negative effect on children's behaviour across the board, not just those prone to hyperactivity or allergies. The findings of this report detailed that all the 3-year-olds involved in the study reacted negatively to benzoates, but some were more sensitive than others, reacting at a lower dose. This confirmed that reactions to these preservatives are *dose related and cumulative*, making it extremely difficult for people to make the connection between health or behaviour problems and benzoate consumption until the additives are removed from the diet completely and then retested.

Children today are consuming more benzoate preservatives than ever before. Benzoates are now being used by manufacturers more and more in drinks other than soft drinks and cordials. They are now found commonly in fruit juices, sports drinks and many water substitutes which are marketed directly at children and school canteens, meaning that more and more children are consuming these additives on a regularly or daily basis in drinks which are perceived by the children and parents as "healthy" choices.

Benzoates have also been linked more recently to another seriously worrying side effect that is of concern to us all, not just asthmatics or children. In 2006 it was revealed that authorities in the USA and UK had found disturbing levels of cancer causing *benzene* residue in many popular brands of soft drink. Following on from the alarming findings overseas, FSANZ conducted some testing of drinks in Australia. Their report confirmed that of the 68 samples tested, 38 had benzene levels from 1-40 ppb, meaning that **more than half** the drinks tested had benzene levels well above the Australian guidelines for drinking water of 1ppb.

Benzene is a nasty chemical linked to cancers, particularly leukaemia. It can form in soft drinks that contain two specific ingredients: Vitamin C (ascorbic acid), and either sodium benzoate or potassium benzoate. Researchers speculate that benzoates can break down in the presence of heat or light into benzene. Regardless of why it is happening, benzene is not something that any of us should be drinking on a regular basis, especially not our children.

In May 2007 yet another red flag emerged in relation to the safety of benzoate preservatives. Research from the University of Sheffield was released claiming that laboratory studies could demonstrate that sodium benzoate could cause serious cell damage at the DNA level. Study head, Professor Peter Piper, released the worrying discovery that benzoates and sorbates are capable of causing extensive damage to an important area of DNA in the power station of cells known as the mitochondria. Speaking in Australia in November 2007 at the *Food Industry and Labelling Conference*, Professor Piper provided the international keynote address on his findings. He stressed that these new results must be investigated further as a matter of priority, as the original safety studies completed on both benzoates and sorbates would not have been able to detect these types of changes due to the limitations of technology at the time.

There is no need to expose yourself or your family to these chemicals in your diet. There are plenty of safe preservatives available which can be used instead of benzoates and sorbates, and there are plenty of good choices on offer in the shops. So have a good look at your fruit juices, cordials and sports drinks and steer clear of products containing benzoates wherever possible.

9.12 Dried fruit and fresh fruit

Most dried fruit is preserved by the use of sulphur dioxide (220) or potassium sorbate (202). Sultanas are often coated in vegetable oil as a preservative, and the oil often contains an unlabelled antioxidant which you may need to ring and check on if you wish to avoid certain antioxidants. Unless you're buying organic dried fruit, you can assume it's preserved by sulphur dioxide, which many people, especially asthmatics, may wish to avoid.

Fresh fruit and nuts are often coated with an additive propylene glycol (1520). This helps to retain the moisture. Propylene glycol is *extremely toxic* and is linked to kidney and liver damage. It is a neurotoxin and linked to central nervous system depression. Either buy organic fruit, or make sure you wash your fruit really well, as there's no way of knowing when you buy fruit from the supermarket whether it has been sprayed with propylene glycol or not.

9.13 Antioxidants

Antioxidants are found widely in our foods in just about all products that contain oil or fat in any form. As we have seen previously, in many cases these additives aren't listed on the labels because they are present in amounts of less than 5% of an ingredient. Unfortunately, their use is so widespread that all small percentages of hidden antioxidants do add up. For many people, this can cause serious adverse health effects.

The worst aspect of the use of suspect antioxidants in our foods is that there are many safe alternatives that could be used by manufacturers, but these are more expensive and so are overlooked in favour of cheaper substances.

Antioxidants 300–309 are all safe and effective, and manufacturers using these antioxidants are to be applauded. However antioxidants 310–312 and 319–321 are *extremely questionable* and should be avoided wherever possible. Apart from their individual toxic characteristics these antioxidants are also suspected of being dangerous to asthmatics.

9.14 Propyl, octyl and dodecyl-gallate (310–312)

These substances are highly irritant to asthmatics and are all prohibited in foods for infants and young children, yet they are commonly found in many foods that children eat on a regular basis. They are known to cause skin irritations and gastric upsets and should also be avoided by those people sensitive to aspirin or salicylates. They are suspected carcinogens and 312 caused death in animal tests. They should all be avoided and especially not given to children or consumed by pregnant and breastfeeding women.

9.15 Tert-butylhydroquinone or TBHQ (319)

This additive is found most often in snack foods and some savoury biscuits as an additive in the oil and is often not labelled. A dose of 5 grams is known to be fatal to an adult, but manufacturers aren't required to list how much of the additive is present in the food. It is a suspected carcinogen and is linked to birth defects. Ingestion can cause nausea, vomiting, delirium and collapse. It should be avoided in particular by infants, young children and pregnant or breastfeeding women.

9.16 Butylated hydroxyanisole or BHA (320)

This is probably the most common of the suspect antioxidants that most people should avoid. It is found widely in sweet and savoury biscuits, margarine, peanut butter, ice-cream cones, frozen foods and mayonnaise, *even though it's prohibited in foods intended for infants and young children.*

It is of particular concern because it accumulates in the body fat, so residual levels increase over time as more and more is consumed. It is a known animal carcinogen and produces detrimental reproductive effects in animal tests. It is a suspected human carcinogen and acts as a xeno-oestrogen (a substance that mimics the effects of oestrogen) stimulating the growth of breast cells in laboratory cultures. Apart from its strong links to cancer, it should be avoided, especially by children, because of its ability to disrupt the body's hormone balance in this way. Recent research in New Zealand is also looking into a possible link between BHA and asthma, in particular the use of this additive in dairy produce such as margarines.

Because of the cumulative effect of BHA, it's worthwhile finding out for sure what you're eating and what you're feeding to your kids.

9.17 Butylated hydroxytoluene or BHT (321)

In experimental animals, BHT has proven to be a teratogen and carcinogen and produces adverse effects on reproductive organs. In rat experiments the number of births decreased as the dose of BHT increased, and it induced benign and malignant growths in the livers. It is strongly suspected of being a human teratogen also. Once again because of such serious health impacts and the possibility that it may contribute to birth defects, it's an additive to be avoided wherever possible, *especially by children and pregnant and breastfeeding women.*

9.18 What should you do?

There are many products available today that use the "good" antioxidants, and these are the ones we want to support. We also want to send a loud message to those other manufacturers that we, as consumers, don't want to eat toxic substances in our food. We can best provide this feedback by not supporting those companies using suspect antioxidants to save themselves a dollar at the expense of our health.

Unfortunately, because of the 5% labelling loophole, there are many, many products on the supermarket shelves that contain undeclared antioxidants. If you don't want to eat these suspect chemicals in your food, you'll need to make a few phone calls to check with the manufacturers of any products you buy that have oils or fats in their ingredient lists.

Chapter 10: So what's left?

10.1 Decision time

Having read this far, you're probably either feeling really motivated to reduce your intake of certain additives or else you're feeling overwhelmed and a bit depressed about what this new knowledge might mean to your eating habits.

Well don't despair — it's really not that hard to make a few very simple changes to your eating habits that will greatly reduce your exposure to harmful additives and improve your health.

The first thing you need to do is to decide which additives you want to avoid. This will depend upon your own health and circumstances, but a summary list of the most concerning additives is provided in *Appendix 1* on page 101 for your reference. For example, if asthma isn't a problem in your family then you may not be too concerned about sulphites and some preservatives. Alternately, you may decide that you want to eliminate all additives with *any* known adverse health effects from your diet.

Even if you don't have any specific health concerns at the moment, it makes sense for each of us to make some informed decisions about the food we eat and feed our families. As we have seen previously, the amount of additives we're all consuming every day has grown exponentially over the past 50 years.

A recent study in the UK estimated that by age 18, most children would have consumed half their body weight in food additives.

Knowing what we now know about the potential toxicity of many of these additives, this has to be concerning. Making a decision to reduce your family's intake of all suspect additives may not have an immediately obvious benefit, but it can only do your family's health good to eat less additives, especially those with question marks surrounding their long term safety.

The very good news is that choosing low-additive foods doesn't mean boring foods. In the main, there are better low-additive choices across all the main product ranges, so in many cases you can still eat the same sort of food, just a different brand. For a clear example of how you can shop smarter and pick the best brands to drastically reduce your additive intake, have a look at the *Additive Consumption Comparison table* on Page 92.

Remember though, that junk is still junk, and highly processed and refined snack foods should not feature prominently in a good, healthy-eating plan anyway. We should be trying to eat less processed and packaged food and more fresh food. In this way, you'll avoid a great number of unnecessary additives in your diet.

Deciding to go low additive doesn't mean that another barbecue-flavoured corn chip or chocolate biscuit will never pass your lips. What this does mean is that you'll choose to eat these foods much less frequently than before, and when you do eat them, you'll be well aware of what you're doing and what's in the food you're eating.

10.2 Changing the habits of a lifetime

The guiding principle in making long-term dietary change is to take it slowly. Don't feel as if you have to empty out your pantry and fridge and restock everything from scratch. If you try to do this, you'll probably get overwhelmed and give up, and it will cost you a fortune.

Approach the change *gradually*, and you'll be much more likely to make changes that you'll stick to and which will become your normal eating habits within a very short time.

Focus on becoming aware of what you're eating now, identify the most important changes to make, and change your product choices accordingly, bit by bit.

How to start changing the habits of a lifetime

- Start with your staples like bread, margarine, cereals, biscuits, juice, canned foods, lunchmeats and fillings, and cooking sauces.

- Have a quick look at the labels of the brands you buy and see if they contain the things you now know you want to avoid.

- If they do, pick one item at a time, then next time you need to restock that item, allow a little extra time to read the labels of just that one product and find a better choice.

It may take a few weeks, but it's better to do it bit by bit than to take on too much and give up. By making the changes gradually, as you need to restock items, you'll find that you very quickly end up with better choices in your house, at the very least for the staple foods you eat every day.

Once you have sorted out your staple grocery choices, do the same with the other products you buy every week. It may seem like a big task at first, but if you approach it systematically like this, it will only be a few weeks until you have found better brands for most things, and you'll have eliminated a huge amount of unnecessary, possibly dangerous additives from your everyday diet.

By opting for the best low-additive products, you can still buy yummy chocolate biscuits, but you might choose *Arnott's Caramel Crowns,* with no suspect additives, over *Arnott's Tim Tams,* which contain five colours.

You might choose *Savings Margarine,* with no suspect additives, over *Flora Canola,* which contains two preservatives and two colours.

For ice cream, you might choose *Sara Lee French Vanilla Ice Cream*, with no additives, over *Signature Range Vanilla*, which contains six additives.

It's all a matter of choice, and with the information you now have, it's easy to make the good choices.

Chapter 11: Healthier low-additive eating guidelines

11.1 Introduction

We all know that we should be eating more fruit and vegetables and that most of us don't eat enough whole foods. With the current obesity crisis facing Australia, as in most western countries, governments and health officials are trying hard to educate us all about better eating to try to turn around the worrying trend towards obesity, especially amongst our children. However being educated about what we should eat and translating that into practice are two entirely different matters.

As a nation, we don't eat our two fruit and five vegetables every day, and we eat far too much processed food. We eat too much salt and sugar and nowhere near enough fibre. The changes in our dietary habits over the past 50 years reflect the ever increasing pace of our lives, and therein lies a big problem when it comes to additives

Busy lives mean less time. It means people want convenient food that looks good, tastes good, is quick to cook and lasts a long time. The cost of such convenience is a staggering blow to our overall health and nutrition and a huge increase in the consumption of additives every day.

Here are some basic shopping and eating principles that are simple to adopt but which can make a big difference to our overall health and wellbeing. In the main, these changes won't cost you anything, but they may make a huge difference to your health in the long run. All you need is a desire to eat better and the dedication to use the information you now have to your best advantage.

11.2 Increase your fruit and vegetable consumption

We all should eat at least two fruit and five vegetables a day but how many of us do? This is one thing you really should work on. Even if you can't get up to two and five, at least aim to improve by 50% whatever you manage now.

Try to get one fruit in with your breakfast (and don't skip breakfast!) and another in as a snack throughout the day. Eating five vegetables is easy to achieve if you just plan your meals. Try to get some salad in with your lunch and at least three sorts of vegies on your plate for the evening meal.

Be creative with kids, and hide them if you have to. (The vegies, not the kids!) Grate some zucchini and carrot inside an omelette. Add some mashed, cooked vegies to sausage rolls. Add veggies to your pizza toppings, and only allow tinned spaghetti if it has some vegies mixed in with it.

There are lots of good cookbooks out to help with ideas so have a look at some if you need some inspiration to improve your family's intake.

11.3 Go organic if you can

Organic food is often more expensive, but it tastes so much better and is so much better for you. If you can afford it, go the whole way with organic everything including fruit and vegetables, meats, eggs and grains. If that's too expensive, at least try to choose organic fruit and vegies to reduce your exposure to pesticide residues that are present in our supermarket foods at disturbing levels.

The main factor stopping people from choosing organic produce is often financial, as we tend not to prioritise our own health unless we're already sick.

Think hard about the wisdom of saving a dollar now at the expense of your long-term health. It may well be far more economic in the long run to spend a little more on good quality food for your family now and possibly avoid health problems in the future.

Even if you don't put your own health first, think hard about at least sourcing organic produce for your children, especially during the first five years of life. Remember that, dose for weight, children are impacted far more than an adult by the pesticide residues in non-organic produce.

Research shows that populations that eat organic food have significantly less (only 10 – 20%) of the residual pesticides in their bodies compared to those who eat regular produce that is pesticide treated. In addition, organic foods have much higher nutrient levels than regular produce, so although you may pay a little more, you get a lot more nutrition from your food.

If you can't stretch to organic fruit and vegetables, at least make sure you wash your produce *really* well to try to limit your intake of contaminants.

11.4 Drink more water

You should aim to drink six to eight glasses of water every day, not including tea and coffee. It should be filtered water if possible.

There is a huge variety of filtration systems available ranging from very inexpensive bench-top jugs to sophisticated reverse-osmosis systems. Find a system that suits your needs, and your budget, and start enjoying the taste and benefits of pure fresh water.

11.5 Eliminate fizzy drinks and cordials

Kids today are drinking an amazing amount of fizzy drink as part of their normal daily diet. Some kids have a can of Coke before school everyday. Apart from the high sugar content (or worse, the effects of artificially sweetened drinks) these drinks are also full of colours and preservatives.

Many adults also consume several cans of soft drink a day as part of their normal diet. Aside from the effects of the colours, sweeteners and preservatives contained in them, excessive consumption of cola drinks is also linked to bone deterioration from the leaching of calcium. This is especially worrying in growing children.

These drinks are intended to be consumed occasionally, not every day. Once, they were consumed only at parties or special occasions. Somehow, they have become a feature of our everyday diet. Learn to drink water again, and get your kids drinking water or diluted, additive-free fruit juice.

Water quenches your thirst better than any soft drink will. Keep the soft drink in reserve for parties and special occasions. At the very least, greatly restrict its consumption in your house.

Cordials also are the staple drink of many kids, but they too are full of colours and preservatives of which kids don't need regular daily doses. Again, eliminate them if you can. Replace them with diluted fruit juice or, preferably, water. At the very least, restrict their consumption in your house.

11.6 Choose no-additive juices

Many of us start each day with a glass of fruit juice, but how many of us realise that this healthy start to our day contains several artificial colours and preservatives?

Most of the cheaper fruit-juice-blend drinks containing 35% juice are the worst culprits. Unfortunately, because they are often cheaper, they are the most popular choice for many Mums trying to keep costs down.

Try, instead, to choose 100% juices. These, in the main, don't have colours and preservatives added. If cost is a concern, try diluting them with water to make them go further. Even better, buy a juicer and make your own fresh juices. These taste fantastic and are very good for you.

Small "juice poppers" have become a lunch-box favourite for school kids. Again, most of these contain little fruit juice and lots of colours such as Tartrazine (102), Sunset Yellow (110), Brilliant Blue (133) and preservatives including potassium sorbate (202) and sodium metabisulphite (223). These are all additives linked with undesirable health effects.

You can buy additive-free poppers, or make up a drink of diluted juice or plain water to go in the lunch boxes. The appeal of these poppers is they are a convenient size and kids like them, but don't be a sucker for marketing and trends. Avoid these products, and remove another dose of unnecessary harmful additives from your kids' diet.

11.7 Bread

It is the use of calcium proprionate (282) in bread that is of most concern. As discussed earlier, this additive is linked to a wide range of adverse health effects. It is considered one of the most insidious additives as it's contained widely in one of our staple foods that we all regard as healthy. It affects adults and children but also affects babies exposed through breast milk, resulting in gastric upsets and pain, irritability, constant crying and sleep disturbances.

Unfortunately its use is so widespread that it's getting difficult to find products that don't use it. As of May 2004, both *Brumby's* and *Bakers Delight* advise that their breads don't contain this additive, and some supermarket lines such as *Helga's, Noble Rise* and *Burgen* say they also don't use it.

There are, of course, organic varieties that are preservative free but more expensive. Alternately, you can buy a preservative-free premix, such as Lauckes, and bake your own.

If you want to also avoid antioxidants 310–329, you need to check your bread label to see if it contains vegetable oil in the mix. If it does, you'll need to ring the enquiry line and check about antioxidants as they will probably not be declared on the label.

As at January 2004, *Bakers Delight* state that their bread doesn't contain 319 or 320 anymore.

11.8 Butter, margarine and spreads

Since the 1970s, there's been a sustained awareness campaign to alert consumers to the dangers of excessive fat consumption and links to high cholesterol and heart disease. Since then the consumption of margarines and spreads other than butter have soared, but the rates of heart disease have not come down. Heart disease remains the leading cause of death amongst Australians.

Obviously just switching to margarine hasn't been the answer to reduce cholesterol and heart disease. Why? Basically because we just eat too much of it and other fats. Rather than just eating less butter and fat, we switched to margarine and continued to over-use it believing it was better for us.

The truth is that margarine isn't necessarily a healthier food than butter. Margarine is a very unnatural product. It is a *hydrogenated fat*. This is a vegetable oil that has been processed to become saturated and in this process the essential fatty acids are destroyed. What remains is an artificial, solid fat that is very long lasting, great for convenience, but at what cost to our health?

Margarine is high in *trans fatty acids* (TFAs). These are dangerous substances known to contribute to higher cholesterol levels and the formation of carcinogenic substances. Be aware that trans fats aren't just in the margarine you buy, but they are also present in large amounts in just about any processed food containing hydrogenated fat or oil as an ingredient.

Our consumption of these substances has increased 50-fold over the past 20 years, and they are getting very difficult to avoid. If you buy packaged cakes, biscuits, most breads, frozen meals and any commercially fried foods (to name just a few), you'll be consuming large amounts of trans fats in your diet every day.

Unfortunately, even if you do want to read labels to avoid these substances, the labelling in Australia is still not as rigorous as in some other countries in relation to trans fats. In Europe today, trans fats are severely restricted with some countries permitting no more than 0.1% in food products. In some countries, including Denmark and Holland, some of the types of margarine sold in Australia would be outlawed, and anything with trans fatty acids in it must state the levels on the label. In Australia, it's only mandatory for manufacturers to declare the total amount of fat and provide a breakdown of the amount of saturated fat. Manufacturers only have to provide a breakdown of trans fats if there's some claim in respect of cholesterol or trans fats.

In addition to this, margarines also usually contain several preservatives, colours and antioxidants to make them last even longer. The antioxidants used are often the most suspect ones including 310 and 320, and they often don't appear on the label. Some margarines and spreads now even contain flavour enhancers, especially the lite and low salt varieties. As the products have less taste, enhancers are included to improve the flavour.

So, in the quest for better health, we have gone from eating too much of a natural substance to eating too much of a totally artificial, very unhealthy substance full of additives and trans fats. It is, therefore, no surprise that our health as a nation hasn't improved as a result.

The healthier approach is to choose the *more natural, unadulterated foods.* Butter is good in moderation, but most of us want to eat too much of it. Butter has no additives or trans fats, but is high in saturated fats, so too much isn't a good idea.

In moderation, however, butter is a better choice than margarine. If you still prefer margarine, try to find one with no harmful additives and the lowest amount of trans fats.

If you want to stay with butter but reduce your butter intake, here are some very simple changes to make:

* Have porridge, muesli or cereal for breakfast most of the time rather than toast. This way you won't need butter in the morning.

- Halve the amount of butter you use on sandwiches or start using avocado, olive oil, tahini, nut butter or ricotta cheese as a base spread for your sandwiches.

- If you're having mayonnaise on your sandwich, don't use any butter.

Just these simple changes will greatly reduce your daily intake of butter, and you'll be avoiding several doses of unsafe additives that you'd have consumed from eating most margarines.

As a general guideline, we should aim to eat mostly mono-unsaturated and polyunsaturated fats and minimise our intake of saturated and trans fats.

It's recommended that non-overweight adults aim for a daily total of no more than 60 grams of fat with a maximum of 20 grams of saturated fat. Those who need to lose weight should keep to a total of no more than 30–50 grams of fat per day with a maximum of 10–15 grams of saturated fat.

11.9 Low fat and lite products

With soaring obesity rates, it's no surprise that there's a huge consumer interest in products that claim to be low fat or lite. Unfortunately, as with the butter example above, it isn't really a matter of *what* we eat, but rather how *much* we eat of certain foods. People love a quick fix, and nobody really likes dieting or limiting their favourite foods. Really though, the problem isn't with full-fat products such as regular ice cream or biscuits, per se. It is just that, overall, we eat too many high fat, high sugar products, and this is the habit we should be changing.

Low fat and lite products, in general, are very unnatural, highly processed products. Often, to make these products lite, a percentage of the fat content is removed. This means the product doesn't taste as good as its full-fat counterpart, so extra sugar or artificial sweeteners and flavour enhancers are added to make them taste more like the real thing. Reducing fat content often leads to changes in colour or texture also, so artificial colours, thickeners and gums are added to improve the appearance and bulk up a watery low-fat product.

Remember also that a product marketed as low fat or lite doesn't necessarily mean low kilojoule. If they have added more sugar to improve the taste after removing the fat, you may be getting just as many empty kilojoules from the product as you'd have got from eating the same amount of the normal product.

This weight-conscious market is a huge cash cow for food manufacturing companies, as people will believe what a label claims, and not too many read the fine print.

Don't be fooled into believing that low fat or lite necessarily means healthier or better for you.

Eating these highly altered foods often means a much higher intake of unnecessary additives in your diet every day. The smarter thing to do is to try to stick to foods that are as close as possible to their natural state. If you do choose the lite varieties, take the time to find ones that are lite *and* low in additives.

There are some good choices that make sense, such as low-fat milk and some yoghurts and cheeses, but avoid the low-fat products swimming in additives, especially sweeteners and flavour enhancers that make up for their lack of taste, texture or colour.

Switching to low fat and lite will not, in itself, cure a weight problem or improve health if the ratio of foods is still out of balance. A healthy diet needs to be high in natural, unprocessed foods and low in sweets and treats. Think about how much of the processed packaged "lite" foods you eat, and concentrate on eating less of them and more fresh fruit, nuts and natural foods.

11.10 Salt

Over the past 30 years, there's also been a great improvement in our awareness about the negative health effects of too much salt in our diets. As a nation we have responded, and studies confirm that we do tend to add less salt to our foods at home than we did 30 years ago, but we are still eating far too much. How can this be? Because we're buying it already added to our foods at the supermarket every week.

Our consumption of processed and packet foods has increased steadily over the past 30 years as a reflection of our busy lives, and we now find that the salt is included in our processed foods in very high concentrations.

The average recommended intake of salt per adult per day is no more than 2.5 grams of sodium. As a guide, one teaspoon of salt has 2 grams of sodium. So, just over a teaspoon of salt per day is the maximum for an adult, and children should have no more than a third of this amount. What we find, though, is that most of us eat far more than that every day and only about a third of what we eat comes from the salt shaker. The rest is hidden in the processed foods that make up a high proportion of our diet.

Sodium contents are surprisingly high in even staple foods such as bread and cheese. Two slices of average wholemeal bread contain about 500 milligrams of sodium, and 30 grams of processed cheddar cheese contains 400 milligrams of sodium, so a child having a cheese sandwich for lunch could be exceeding his daily sodium allowance without eating anything else!

The main culprits, however, are breakfast cereals, canned foods, canned soups, sauces, cooking sauces, flavour bases, packet soups and frozen meals.

It makes a big difference choosing low-salt varieties of products such as baked beans and spaghetti. Half a cup of canned spaghetti contains an average of 570 milligrams of salt but a salt reduced variety can contain as little as 40 milligrams. Some pasta stir-through sauces (enough for two servings) contain 2,500 milligrams of salt and most brands of tomato sauce contain 200 milligrams in just one tablespoon.

Breakfast cereals are another area to look at carefully. A recent Health Department survey in Western Australia revealed that a serve of *Rice Bubbles* has a whopping 72 times the sodium level of *Quick Oats*. Frozen foods are another potent source of hidden sodium that varies greatly from brand to brand. *Logan Farm Crinkle Cut Oven Fries* contain only 3 milligrams of sodium per 100 grams; whereas, *Birds Eye Golden Crunch Fries* contain 100 times more.

Unlike the low fat and lite products discussed previously, it makes good sense to shop for no-salt, low salt and salt-reduced products wherever possible, especially for children. Most kids in Australia consume more salt than most adults should have every day. Labels will give you sodium content per 100 grams, so have a look and go for the low-salt choices, preferably those containing no more than 120 milligrams of sodium per 100 grams.

11.11 Sugar

We nibble our way through mountains of sugar every year, and in 1997–98 Australians consumed on average around 42 kilograms of sugar *each,* according to the Australian Bureau of Statistics report *Apparent Consumption of Foodstuffs Australia (Cat No 4306.0).*

Many people will find this statistic horrifying, and remember it's an *average*, so if you believe that you don't consume your 42 kilograms every year this means that some other Australian is consuming more — most probably a child! In light of this, it really isn't any wonder that obesity and diabetes are two of the biggest health issues facing our society today.

So although we may have cut down on the amount of sugar we add to our food and drinks, it's sneaking into our diets, pre-mixed for our convenience by the manufacturers. It is in the obvious sources such as biscuits, cakes, yoghurts, ice creams and soft drinks, but also in less obvious sources such as fruit juice, sauces and marinades, mayonnaise, breakfast cereals, canned foods and frozen meals.

The labels will confess to how much sugar is in a product, so if you don't want to eat another 42 kilograms of sugar this year, have a look at what's in your weekly shopping and get rid of the brands with high sugar contents. As an easy guide, remember that 5 grams is about equal to 1 teaspoon of sugar. It doesn't matter at all if it is sucrose, fructose or glucose – it is all still sugar. As a very loose rule, aim for products which contain no more than 15g per 100gm of sugar in total. Some fruit juices and fruit bars are the worst culprits for excess sugar with many popular fruit bars and muesli bars containing up to 15gm of sugar in each 20gm bar!!

Again, just by reverting as much as possible to foods in their most natural state and avoiding processed and packaged products, you'll eliminate many products high in sugar. In the process, you'll be doing your body a huge health favour.

In May 2004, the WA Health Department released a survey of well-known cereals to show how much sugar, salt and fibre are in the most popular brands. The results showed that many popular brands such as *Rice Bubbles* and *Nutrigrain* have incredibly high levels of salt and sugar, despite the public perception created by slick marketing that they are relatively healthy foods.

Have a look at the labels on the packets in your pantry. Inform yourself, and make a better choice next time you go shopping.

11.12   Whole grains

In combination with our over consumption of saturated fats, salt and sugar, as a nation we also don't eat enough whole grains. Our favourite choices are white bread, white rice and pasta. Combined with our under consumption of fresh fruit and vegies, we don't get enough fibre.

The simplest way to introduce more whole grains into your diet is to switch today to wholemeal bread. (Not white bread with grains in it — wholemeal made with wholemeal flour.) It has much more taste that white bread, and kids will get used to it if you insist on the change.

Look also at your breakfast cereals. Many of the most popular brands have almost negligible fibre content and are more confectionary than cereal. This is an easy avenue to increase the dietary fibre intake for the whole family. The best way to do this is to start eating porridge or untoasted muesli for breakfast. (Watch out for high sugar contents in some commercial brands.)

If your family has to stay with the highly processed cereals, at least choose the varieties with the highest fibre and lower salt and sugar contents such as *Weet Bix* and *All Bran*. If you can't get the family to switch completely, at least restrict the rations of the junky brands to once a week or mix some of the higher fibre varieties on top. Just a little bit can make a big difference.

Another good idea is to sprinkle Linseed, Sunflower and Almond mix (LSA) on top of your cereal. This is just ground up nuts available in supermarkets and health-food stores and is an excellent source of fibre, essential fats, vitamins and minerals. This is a great habit to get your kids into.

Next, start to eat brown rice instead of white, at least some of the time. It takes a little longer to cook, but it does have a delicious nutty flavour and goes well with all dishes. You can also switch to wholemeal pasta and can start to introduce some legumes into your diet; e.g. chickpeas, beans and lentils. Australians on the whole eat far too few of these highly nutritious, fibre-packed foods, but they are quite easy to incorporate into your diet. Chickpeas and beans (fresh or canned) are great, easy additions to salads, stews and especially curries.

Eat more nuts and dried fruit (organic if possible). These healthy foods are great for snacks instead of biscuits and snack bars, and provide another easy way to boost your fibre intake. Stay away from breakfast bars and fruit rollups. These are little more than lollies often with up to 60% sugar content.

Implementing just these simple changes will reap important overall health benefits for your whole family. Even if you don't make a complete change to whole grains, improving by at least 50% on what you do now will be significant.

11.13 Cooking sauces and flavour bases

One of the many by-products of our busier lifestyles has been the advent of the instant cooking sauces and flavour base sachets. The range is huge: *Maggi Cook in the Pot, Chicken Tonight, Dolmio Sauces, Continental Easy Meals, Kantong Stir Through Sauce* and many, many more. Because they make a tasty sauce and because they let us whip up a meal very easily, they are favourites with many people, especially busy families.

Amazingly, though, once these one-pot wonders did not exist, yet families 50 years ago still enjoyed tasty stews, casseroles, pasta, stir fry and curries. How did they do it? Easily, you see, because people used to cook, not just open a packet or jar. If you want to avoid a large source of questionable additives in your diet, you need to look carefully at your use of these ready-made sauces (and also the instant noodle and pasta sauce products), upon which many of us have come to rely as weekly standards in our diet.

"Oh no", I hear you groan. "That's going to be too hard. I don't have time to make this change! I haven't got time to cook a meal from scratch!" Relax, it's not that hard, and once you have a look at the additives that make some of these products so tasty, I doubt you'll want to be feeding them to your family every night anyway.

Although it's best to cook your own and steer away from these convenience ranges, once again there's good news for those of you who can't imagine cooking dinner without a jar or a packet. Across most of these product ranges, there are again good and bad choices.

I used to rely heavily on sauces and packet mixes for all my staple dishes. It was a habit borne out of being busy, and I was amazed when I had a close look at what's in these things. Apart from horrific salt levels in a lot of these products, the reason a lot of these products taste so good is because of the heavy use of flavour enhancers 620 to 637. Many also add colours, especially Caramel (150), which has a question mark hanging over its long term safety.

You can still keep some of these products in the pantry for weekend standbys and those nights when you need something quick and easy, but just take the time to make sure they are the ones with no harmful additives.

For example, you may choose *Continental Chicken Tonight Pasta Bake*, which has no suspect additives, instead of their *Stroganoff Simmer Sauce,* which contains 627 and 150.

Similarly, most of the *Kantong Stir Through Sauce* range is okay, except for a few which contain Caramel (150). *Continental Easy Meals Apricot Chicken Curry* has no suspect additives, but their *Chicken Tomato Red Wine Casserole* contains Caramel (150) and two flavour enhancers (635 and 627) that you may decide to avoid.

As you can see, it isn't hard to find products with few or no additives. Although it's preferable to cook your dishes with fresh ingredients, you don't have to swear off these convenience products totally. With a little awareness, you can still enjoy the convenience factor, but make sure you avoid exposing your family to numerous servings of suspect additives just by choosing the varieties with less additives.

A word of warning, though, about hidden additives in cooking sauces. Many of these products have vegetable oil as an ingredient, so many contain antioxidants that aren't listed. During the research for this book I found that many use 310, 319 and 320, so if these are additives you want to avoid, you may need to make a couple of phone calls to the manufacturer to help finalise which products you choose and which ones you avoid.

11.14 Two-minute noodles and pasta snacks

Observing people at the checkouts whilst researching this book, I was astounded at the volume of two-minute noodles and similar products many families buy. The bad news is that none of these products are good choices additive wise. Even the noodles themselves are sometimes not okay with many popular brands containing colours and antioxidant 319 in the actual noodles, and the flavour sachets are all laden with MSG, flavour enhancers, colours and salt.

If your kids are hooked on these, start wreaking some changes at your house because these are not good food for anyone, especially not kids.

A tasty alternative is to buy plain noodles made from wheat, flour and salt (*Fantastic* is a brand I use), cook them, drain them and gently heat them through with some additive free tomato sauce or soy sauce and honey. This might take you three minutes, not two, but it's a healthier alternative.

Instant pasta sauce meals are also a product range which, on the whole, are chock full of too much salt, flavour enhancers, suspect antioxidants and colours. There are definitely some varieties that are better than others, but these products should be seen as very occasional side dishes, not complete meals, and should not feature as a regular part of your diet. Like two-minute noodles, many people favour these convenient "meals" for the kids under the mistaken impression that they are a relatively healthy choice. They are not.

A far healthier alternative would be to boil some pasta and toss through some cold chicken, tomato, ricotta and grated cheese. This honestly doesn't take any more time than it takes to open the packet and cook it in the microwave, but it's a far superior choice healthwise.

11.15   Avoid processed meats

This is a big one, especially for children who consume probably more processed meats on average in their school lunches every day than most adults. Meats such as ham, polony and salami are all preserved with nitrates or nitrites, which are suspected human carcinogens. Many of them also contain several suspect artificial colours.

Even packaged ham these days sometimes contains flavour enhancers and vegetable gums like Carrageenan 407. Other processed meats like chicken loaf are usually full of flavour enhancers and/or MSG. Aside from the additives in them, the fat and salt contents of these products are very high and they should not be featuring as a substantial part of our everyday diet.

It is easy to make some changes to eliminate or greatly reduce your use of these products. The first thing to do is to limit how many times a week you and your family eat these items. If you have to, give the kids a polony (devon) or ham sandwich once a week, not every day.

Our family used to eat a lot of ham and processed meat but we now buy a small amount every 2 weeks and we enjoy maybe one ham sandwich a fortnight. We also buy low nitrate, organic ham which is available through organic food suppliers and more and more butchers as demand grows.

Instead of processed meat, choose different fillings such as cheese or egg and enjoy the variety. Don't buy the one-kilo knobs of polony as it just sits in the fridge to be snacked on and is gone before you know it.

Next, start to enjoy real cold meat again. On the weekend cook up a large chook or a leg of lamb or roast beef in the oven, and keep it in the fridge for sandwiches and snacks for the week ahead. Real roast-meat sandwiches are far nicer than polony or artificial chicken roll and contain less salt, less fat and no additives. For yourself, but especially for your kids, this simple change will eliminate a considerable amount of unsafe additives from the daily diet.

11.16 Party food

Once you become aware of the number of carcinogens and other questionable substances that are in our food, it's hard to look at a children's party table laden with frankfurts, fairy bread and *Cheezels* the same way. Even as parents who generally try to limit junk intake by their kids, we still allow them to feast on these foods on special occasions such as birthdays, even though we know this food is no good for them. With what you now know, doesn't that seem like a crazy thing to do?

After working so hard to eliminate so many additives from my family's diet, I was determined not to do the party additive binge again for my daughter's third birthday. I have proven that it's possible to have very successful children's birthday parties with few or no suspect additives on the menu.

The very interesting thing after this party was the number of comments that came back from the parents about how happy and well behaved the thirteen little kids raging around inside on a rainy day had been. Everyone had a good time and they didn't go home hyped up, irritable and wrecked. It was a convincing moment for me that additives in food have a very real, observable effect on many (if not most) children. Some just more than others.

So for the next kids' party make a decision not to dose your kids up on chemicals. Try these tasty alternatives and enjoy the difference:

- Make mini meatballs and homemade sausage rolls instead of frankfurts.

- Have plain potato chips and lightly salted corn chips instead of flavoured chips and cheese snacks.

- Try Nutella bread not fairy bread.

- Chocolate crackles and pikelets are always a hit.

- Make a real chocolate cake with cocoa, not with five or six different carcinogenic colours as found in many of the packet and store bought cakes.

- Decorate the cake with Maltesers and white marshmallows instead of Smarties and jelly beans.

- Have some healthy sandwiches and fruit and cheese platters available too.

- Lollies for the lolly bags can contain white and chocolate Freddo Frogs, Maltesers, Milk Bottles, honeycomb squares, natural liquorice, and the Natural Confectionary Company's snakes, jellies and jubes.

Simple changes such as this will be unnoticed by the kids. They will still have a great time and enjoy their party food, and you may well find you have some very grateful parents at the end of the party.

11.17   Foods for young children

As parents, one of the most important things we can do for our children is to set them up with healthy eating habits from an early age. This means starting from the time of their first foods and continuing the good choices throughout their childhood.

Most women are extremely careful about what they eat and drink during pregnancy and breastfeeding to protect their baby. Unfortunately, however, as children grow and start to eat a wider variety of foods, parents often unwittingly make some very poor choices. Many of these choices are guided by the aggressive marketing of the food manufacturers that convince us that their products are good healthy choices for our children when, in fact, they are not. Their marketing makes us feel good about their foods when, in fact, their food may be damaging our children's health.

We have discussed earlier the negative effects of substances like MSG and Aspartame, and the ability of these additives to impact the developing foetus. These additives are capable of causing damage to the brain development of young animals and disrupting the endocrine (hormone) system later in life. As such, they should be *avoided by women during pregnancy and breastfeeding, and should not be fed to young children at all.*

The human brain continues to grow for three years after birth, and there are many critical phases of development throughout this time.

Unfortunately, from the age of two, or even younger in some cases, children are being allowed to eat foods containing these substances regularly. Foods such as chips, savoury biscuits, flavoured rice crackers, tinned meals, processed meats, instant noodles and pasta snacks feature prominently in many children's diets. These same foods are promoted as good choices by food manufacturers.

Even worse, these products are often made more appealing to parents through the use of convenient kid-size packaging. *You cannot rely on the food manufacturers to tell you what's good for your child.* Take a stand. Take charge of your children's health, and stop buying these products for your kids. They are definitely not good for them nutritionally, and they may well be doing them real, long-term harm.

Remember when starting your child on solid food, that you have a blank canvas to work with. It is very much within your control to shape your child's tastes and eating habits for the rest of their life. Don't add salt or sugar to any of their foods as their tastebuds are very sensitive. Even if their food appears bland to you, it will taste great to them just as it is.

Cook your own baby food using organic ingredients if possible, and only use tinned baby foods for occasional meals if you have to. There are organic varieties of baby food readily available in supermarkets and health-food stores, so choose them if you can to avoid your baby eating products containing pesticide residues.

Be very careful also of any baby foods with *vegetable oils* listed as an ingredient as some may contain antioxidants which aren't on the label. During the research for this book I discovered that a leading brand of baby food had previously contained antioxidant 320 in many of its products that contained vegetable oil. This additive is *specifically banned in foods for infants and young children*, yet it had been in circulation in these baby-food products for many years!

This manufacturer now advises that, as of December 2003, their products no longer contain any vegetable oil and therefore no antioxidant 320. This is good, but the question remains: *why this was allowed to go on for so long?*

As your baby grows and you start to introduce more foods, stay well clear of the high additive, high trans fats, processed foods that many kids get hooked on from the age of about two.

In particular, be wary of junky breakfast cereals, MSG-laden savoury biscuits, chips, rice crackers, two-minute noodles, pasta snacks with MSG, popper fruit-juice drinks, brightly coloured foods, white bread and processed meats. These are not good foods for anyone, but especially not for young children.

Even if your child is already eating these things, you can change their diet. You are the parent; you are in charge. Just make changes slowly, one at a time, and you'll gain a great sense of satisfaction as you make the healthy changes and watch your child start to enjoy real food once again.

11.18 Smarter rewards

Be aware also of how you motivate and reward your kids in relation to food. Do you condition them to see a trip to McDonalds or a candy bar as a treat? If you reward and motivate your kids with unhealthy foods, you're sending very mixed messages and promoting these foods as special.

Instead you should be educating your kids that these foods are junk and are bad for us. This doesn't mean you can never take your kids to McDonalds (if you really want to), but make sure that the quality of the food is understood. Ensure they understand that — although they may taste good and it's okay to have them occasionally — these things aren't meant to be eaten every day.

Many of us have grown up with the same poor conditioning, and we pass it on to our kids without even thinking about it. However, if you have young children, you can change the pattern. If you wish to reward or motivate your child, think of rewards other than fast food or lollies. Maybe they can choose an exotic piece of fruit from the greengrocers, a fresh soft bun from the bakery, or a muffin from the health food store.

Even better, get food out of the equation and reward them with a small toy or a book or, better still, *your time*. For young children, this is what they want most anyway.

Reward them with an extra story, a trip to the park or 15 minutes of your undivided attention to play whatever game they choose. Even if your kids already see fast food and junk food as treats, you can start to "recondition" them just by using these rewards less often and introducing new healthier rewards for your family to enjoy.

You can still buy ice creams and lollies for treats if you want to, but apply your knowledge of good and bad additives in your choices. If you choose a *Chocolate Billabong* instead of a *Bubblegum Paddlepop*, you'll avoid several questionable colours. Likewise, choose a white or chocolate *Freddo Frog* instead of ones with colours in the middle, or choose *Maltesers* instead of *Smarties*. Simple changes like this will go practically unnoticed by your children but will eliminate a lot of unnecessary, undesirable additives in their diets.

11.19   Reset your bliss point

Within the food manufacturing industry, there's a term known as the *bliss point*. This refers to enhancing the taste intensity of product to a point that just makes you want to eat more and more. Immediate examples that spring to mind are some corn chips, potato chips and savoury biscuits. Once you start eating them, it's hard to stop.

For all of us, our bliss points are being cranked up higher and higher the more MSG and flavour enhancers we consume. As we eat more artificially flavoured, super-tasty food, we get to like the taste and we go back for more. After a while, normal food tastes bland, so our preferences steer away from natural food to flavour enhanced foods.

Our children's bliss points are being determined at a very early age by the foods they eat, and they are growing up unable to enjoy the taste of plain, healthy food because they have been weaned onto highly flavoured foods from a very early age.

Once you eliminate or greatly reduce your consumption of MSG and other flavour enhancers, you'll be surprised how quickly your bliss point resets itself. High MSG foods that you once used to enjoy and devour in excess will no longer have the same appeal, and you'll find that their taste is too salty and over the top. It really does happen quite quickly once you cut out these additives from your diet. Try it and see for yourself.

The same applies to kids too. If you cut out these foods from their diet, they will complain at first, but stick with it and you'll be amazed that in a very short time they are perfectly happy with plain potato chips or lightly salted corn chips, or additive free rice crackers, rather than MSG laden chips and additive heavy savoury biscuits. This might be hard to imagine, but it will happen once you regain control of your own bliss point and reprogram your kids' tastebuds back to a level closer to that which nature intended.

Chapter 12: Get to it: take control of your kitchen

12.1 Introduction

If you live alone then it's simple to make whatever changes you like to your diet and eating style whenever you like. You only have yourself to consider. If, however, you're a parent or spouse who has to make decisions about what everyone in the family eats, balancing those decisions with everyone's likes and dislikes, it becomes a little more complicated to implement change and maintain a happy household.

Remember, though, ultimately it's *your* kitchen, and if you're the one expected to shop and cook for everyone then you have a big say about these decisions. If you have no kids but your spouse isn't supportive of the changes you want to make, that's fine. Just go ahead and implement the changes you feel are important, and let them shop and cook for themselves for a while. I guarantee you that it won't last long and they will either end up happily eating the healthier low-additive meals you provide, or you'll have half as much shopping and cooking work to do!

If you have children to shop and cook for, though, you may have to prepare yourself for a bit of a battle at first to implement the changes. Even from a very young age, children develop very strong likes and dislikes and are capable of waging sustained defiance campaigns against changes they don't like. Just remember: your children's health and wellbeing is your responsibility. You are the adult and, for quite some time to come, you do know best.

Remember too, that it's one of the most important functions of parenting to lay down good eating habits that will steer your children towards long-term good health. We really only have total control of this area for a few short years. Once they start school, they are influenced from many other directions, and if you cannot gain good control over their eating habits before then, it's going to be extremely hard to instil positive changes down the track.

Many parents have found this when confronted with a health problem such as excess weight, asthma or allergies requiring diet change in the older child. It can be very difficult to undo bad habits that have been laid down in early childhood. If you can instil good patterns before they go to school, you'll be doing their long-term health a huge favour. *We need to prioritise our children's health now, not wait for the problems to emerge later on.*

Take the time, though, to explain your decisions regarding food, even to very young children. From three or four they can understand the concept of good and bad food, and the need to eat well to be strong and healthy. You aren't negotiating, just explaining why the changes are being made. In the process, you're teaching them the foundations for healthier eating patterns throughout their life.

For little children, it's probably easier as they have no other source of income or food. Implement your changes *gradually,* and stick as close as possible to their favourites. Just substitute low-additive varieties and gradually introduce new foods and habits such as more fruit and vegetables, whole grains and healthier cereals.

By going low additive there are certainly individual products that you'll no longer buy, but you can still eat the same sort of food, just better choices. The kids may fuss and carry on for a short time, but dig your heels in and be firm, and it will soon pass. Your family's tastes will very quickly adjust too. Before you know it, the changes will be made and any fuss and bother about it will be a distant memory.

For older children, it's a little more difficult as you cannot control what they spend their pocket money on and what they eat at school. The best advice here is to lead by example and explain to them what you're doing and why. Give them this book to read and take them shopping with you to help pick the best low-additive choices while still enjoying the sorts of food they are used to.

Involve them in cooking and experimenting with recipes without additives which still taste great and, in the process, develop some new favourite family meals. If it makes life easier, you might want to agree to just dramatically reduce some items rather than eliminate them totally from your pantry. For example, you may agree to buy only one bottle of soft drink a week, and decide that it's only drunk on weekends. Agree that one night a week they can cook whatever they like for tea. Don't criticise or try to influence what they choose, even if you don't want to eat it yourself.

Involving older children in setting the framework for the new eating plan is much more likely to succeed than trying to impose unilateral changes "for their own good".

You have to accept that, even if you eliminate the worst additives from your home, your teenager will still probably snack on MSG-laden chips and Coke on the way home from school (possibly for no other reason than just to defy you!), and there's nothing you can do about that. Just be happy in the knowledge that when at home they eat healthy food and they are now eating much less of these harmful additives overall.

Before you start, you may want to take a moment and write down a sample menu for a week of what you and your family eat now for all meals and snacks. Put it away in a safe place then, in six months, after you have made your changes, review it against what your family is eating then.

You may be amazed at the changes, extremely happy at the amount of additives you have eliminated, and astounded at some of the food you used to eat and enjoy, which you now never crave and can't imagine ever buying again.

If you reflect on the general health of your family at the same time, you may well be surprised to find a significant improvement in everybody's health, behaviour and mood.

Have a look now at the following additive-consumption comparison tables to see just how easy it is to make a huge difference to your overall additive intake, just by applying all that you have learnt, shopping smarter and choosing the lower-additive products available in the supermarket.

12.2   Additive consumption comparison

The following tables have been prepared to illustrate clearly how easily the average person can consume large doses of additives as part of an everyday diet. Just by shopping smarter, you can select the lower additive products and dramatically reduce your consumption of all additives, especially those with known or suspected adverse health effects.

The charts that follow compare two similar variations on the menu below, but menu 2, *The Additive Alert Menu*, highlights how easy it is to make safer, low additive choices without changing your food selections greatly.

Breakfast
cereal
muffin with spread and jam
orange juice

Lunch
chicken and cheese sandwich
spread or mayonnaise
yoghurt
biscuit
chocolate milk

Dinner
apricot chicken
savoury rice
chocolate ice cream and apple pie dessert

Additives listed in bold in the following menus have known or suspected adverse health implications. For specific details refer to the "Additive-effects" table presented in *Appendix 4* on page 110.

Breakfast: Standard menu

Breakfast	Additives contained	# of additives linked to health risks
Kellogg's Corn Pops	500 **150 102 110**	3
Buttercup Cheese and Bacon Muffin	472e **200 282 554 621 102 110 150**	7
Country Gold Soft and Light Butter	440 322 470 471 **202 160a 320**	3
Cottees Raspberry Conserve Diet	1200 440a 401 **407** 330 331 **951 202**	3
Daily Juice Co Orange Fruit Drink	330 300 **202 211 160b**	3
Totals	**32 additives**	**19**

Breakfast: Additive Alert menu

Breakfast	Additives contained	# of additives linked to health risks
Kellogg's Corn Flakes		
Tip Top English Muffins	341 **282 200** 481	2
Farmland Butter		
Cottees Raspberry Conserve	440a 330 331	
Crusta Orange Juice Preservative Free		
Totals	**7 additives**	**2**

Lunch: Standard menu

Lunch	Additives contained	# of additives linked to health risks
Buttercup Molenberg Soy and Linseed	471 481 472e 412 **282**	1
Devondale Extra Soft	440 471 **202 220 635 320**	4
Kraft Sweet Chilli Mayonnaise	**1403** 1412 1422 415 330 **320 124 101** 160a	4
Dorsogna Shaved Pressed Chicken	**621** 451 452 316 **223**	2
Kraft Free Singles Cheese Slice	339 341 **220 160b** 171 **200**	3
Nestle Diet Yoghurt Juicy Nectarine	441 **950** 415 412 440 **951 296 202 160b 120** 509	6
Arnott's Tim Tam Chewy Caramel	322 476 422 471 322 **102 110 129 133 150** 503 500	5
Pura Classic Chocolate Flavoured Milk	**407 133 155**	3
Totals	**57 additives**	**28**

Lunch: Additive Alert menu

Lunch	Additives contained	# of additives linked to health risks
Burgen Soy Lin		
Meadow Lea Cholesterol Free Spread	322 471 330 160a	
SW Whole Egg Mayonnaise		
Makers Choice Lightly Smoked Chicken	**223**	1
Mainland Light and Tasty Cheese Slice		
Ski Delite Honey Buzz Yoghurt	441 1442	
Arnotts Scotch Finger Chocolate Biscuits	322 500	
Harvey Fresh Chocolate Milk	471 **407**	1
Totals	**11 additives**	**2**

Dinner: Standard menu

Dinner	Additives contained	# of additives linked to health risks
Gravox Ready Meals Apricot Chicken	1422 **262 621 627 631** 410 471 433 **412 150c** **102 104**	8
Continental Rices Chicken	**621 635 100 150 508**	5
Paul's Extra Cream Chocolate Ice Cream	**102 110 133 150 155** 471 **407** 410 412 466	6
Homebrand Apple Pie	**202 223** 327 471 **102** **122 160b** 306 500 **320** **100** 160a 450 330	7
Totals	**41 additives**	**26**

Dinner: Additive Alert menu

Dinner	Additives contained	# of additives linked to health risks
Continental Apricot Chicken Curry	**150** 415 330	1
Continental Rices Chicken Vegetable	160a **508**	1
Bulla Real Dairy Chocolate Ice Cream	471 412 **407**	1
Nanna's Apple Crumble	1422 500 297 330 410	
TOTALS	**13 Additives**	**3**

Let's compare the total number of additive in the two menus:

Standard menu		Additive Alert menu	
Total # additives		**Total # additives**	
Breakfast	32	Breakfast	7
Lunch	57	Lunch	11
Dinner	41	Dinner	13
Totals	**130**	**Totals**	**31**
Suspect additives		**Suspect additives**	
Breakfast	19	Breakfast	2
Lunch	28	Lunch	2
Dinner	26	Dinner	3
Totals	**73**	**Totals**	**7**

We have reduced the total number of additives in the menu from 130 to 31: a reduction of 76%.

Better still, we have reduced the number of suspect additives from 73 to 7: a reduction of 90%.

You can see from this example just how easy it is to consume a large number of suspect additives in an average day, without even being aware of it.

Conversely, it's just as easy to see how simple it is to dramatically reduce your consumption of additives, especially those with suspect health concerns, with very little effort, just by shopping smarter and choosing the lower-additive alternatives.

Chapter 13: Taking it further by forcing change

If we as consumers want to have our voices heard, there are two main avenues of action open to us. The first is to vote loudly and decisively with our shopping dollars by supporting strongly those manufacturers who supply products with no harmful additives. While we're doing this, the other companies will see their market share dwindle and will start to question why. It won't take them long to work it out. This is probably the most effective method of forcing change as it centres around impacting company profit — and companies watch over and guard their bottom line ferociously.

Voting with your shopping dollar is far more effective, though, when used in conjunction with letter writing or phone calls to tell companies why we're not supporting their products. If you're making a call to check on antioxidants or other hidden additives in a product and you find that a product contains an unsafe additive, tell the operator that you'll not be buying their product because of the additives they use. This information goes back up the line, especially if this type of feedback becomes more and more common, rather than just an occasional call from some poor person with food allergies.

You can also join in the coordinated lobbying which takes place via the Additive Alert online newsletter. Since September 2005 we have been identifying products that contain unnecessary, harmful additives and encouraging people to voice their concerns en masse and request that the manufacturers seek safer alternatives. We now have an ever-growing number of consumers adding their voice to these campaigns and some great successes have resulted already. These coordinated campaigns are sending a very loud and effective message to the manufacturers that Australian consumers demand better performance, and I believe that this type of activity is the fastest path to change. To subscribe to the newsletter and assist in these efforts please just visit the Additive Alert website at **www.additivealert.com.au.**

Manufacturers need to be made aware that it's not just people with actual illnesses or allergies who don't want to eat these chemicals. Everyday, normal, healthy people who are interested in their long-term health and wellbeing also don't want to eat these chemicals, and we need to get this message across. Demand the use of safer alternatives. If enough of us do it, we may see more and more use of the good additives and less and less of the cheap and nasty alternatives that many companies use at the moment.

Sadly, Australia is lagging well behind the trends of many other countries, especially the UK and Europe. Ask anyone who has visited these countries recently and they will confirm that the availability and abundance of additive safe and organic produce is truly startling in comparison to Australia, where such products are often difficult to source and prohibitively expensive to buy. Consumer awareness in Europe about the problems associated with some food additives has driven the manufacturers to take the lead, regardless of what the law demands of them. Following the release of the Southhampton study in September 2007, large manufacturers including Sainsbury's, Tescos and Marks and Spencers were proactive in voluntarily removing many suspect additives from their products, and consumers in the UK consequently have a much easier time finding mainstream groceries that are free from harmful additives.

This should be happening here also, so why is it not? Simply, because manufacturers here are yet to be convinced that this issue is of big enough concern for consumers. It is all about bottom dollar for them and if we consumers are happy to continue to buy products that contain cheap and possibly nasty ingredients, then why would the manufacturers go to the trouble of using more expensive, safer options? Seeing as our regulator is NOT regulating on our behalf, it is unfortunately up to us to drive this change, and we need to do this by communicating directly with the major manufacturers at the checkout, via their feedback lines and though our coordinated lobbying efforts.

The second avenue towards forcing change is to apply sustained pressure on the regulatory authority — in this case Food Standards Australia New Zealand — to change the legislation and protect consumers, as it should. Although it would be nice to imagine that with consumer pressure we could influence FSANZ to ban the use of any food additive with known or suspected adverse health impacts in our food, this isn't a realistic aim in the short term.

However it is totally realistic to believe that with enough consumer pressure we can achieve one very important and fundamental change: *full disclosure in labelling.*

It would be a huge victory for consumers to get rid of the 5% loophole in our legislation, which currently works to the manufacturers' advantage and leaves us in the dark as to what's really in our food. This would be and is the most achievable reform to aim for in the short term.

So how do we make this happen? Simply writing to FSANZ and telling them what we want will be a great start. If FSANZ receives several thousand letters all asking for the same basic change, they will be hard pressed to come up with a compelling reason why it can't be done, especially given that their mandate is *"to protect the health and safety of the people".*

If this is something you'd like to see happen, we've made it easy for you to be part of the process of forcing positive change. At the back of the book is a letter you can use to have your voice heard and demand that FSANZ change the labelling laws to ensure that manufacturers must identify *all* additives in *all* ingredients, no matter how small the percentage.

Either fill in your name and address and sign the letter "as is", or feel free to write your own if you want to say more. For the campaign to be effective, it's critical, though, that all letters consistently ask for the same basic change; i.e. *full disclosure of additives in all ingredients.*

Although it would be nice to demand numerous improvements and changes, to have the maximum chance of success we need to concentrate on one small step at a time.

It would be a powerful start if consumer power could, at the very least, force manufacturers to tell us honestly what's in the food we eat and, thereby, give us the freedom to truly choose what we do and don't wish to eat. This would be a great first step. *If you want to see this happen too, make sure you send off your letter and get your family and friends to do the same by photocopying it or logging onto the website where an electronic version of the petition is available.*

The more letters FSANZ receive asking for the same thing, the harder it will be for them to not act.

Go to it. Let's make a change that counts!

Be aware also that this campaign for truth in labelling is much, much bigger than just the readers of this book. There is a very active campaign for full disclosure in labelling both here in Australia and internationally, and many other countries are far more progressive than Australia.

By sending in this letter, you're not only having your opinion heard, but you'll be supporting a well established push for our rights as consumers to be protected by the agency whose mandate it is to do so.

For more details on other sources associated with truth in labelling, see *Appendix 3, Useful Contacts* on page 106.

Appendix 1: Additives to avoid

Suspected carcinogens

These additives have proven or strongly suspected links to cancer in animals and/or humans.

110 122 123 124 127 129 131 132 133 153 155
249 250 251 252
310 319 320 321
407 407a 431 432 433 435 436 466
553
900 914 943a 950 951 952 954 1201

Additives not recommended for children

Pregnant and breastfeeding women may wish to avoid these also.

102 104 110 120 122 123 124 127 129 131 132 133 142 151 153 155
160b 162
211 216 220 221 222 223 224 225 228 249 250 251 252 264 280 281
282 283 290 296
310 311 312 319 320 321 349 355
405 407 407a 420 421 431 432 433 435 436 466
508 514 553 554 555 556
620 621 622 623 624 625 627 631 635 641
914 943a 943b 944 950 951 952 954 955 956 957 966 967
1201 1520 1521

Prohibited in foods for infants and young children by FSANZ guidelines

Children, pregnant and breastfeeding women may wish to avoid these.

249 250 251 252
310 311 312 320 321
420 421
621 627 631 635

Hyperactive or hypersensitive reaction possible

These should be avoided by children, especially those with ADD or ADHD, or anyone with known chemical sensitivities.

102 103 104 110 120 122 123 124 127 129 131 132 133 142 150 151 155 160b
210 211 220 282
319 320 321
421
620 621 627 631 635
951

Banned in other countries

These additives are still permitted in Australia despite being banned in other countries, often because of their links to cancer, birth defects or other serious safety concerns.

102 104 110 120 122 123 124 127 129 132 133 142 151 153 155 173 174 175
320 385
635
952 954

Linked to asthma

These additives have been known to trigger or exacerbate asthma attacks in sufferers. Asthmatics or anyone at risk of asthma may wish to avoid them.

102 104 110 120 122 123 124 127 129 131 132 133 142 151 155 160b 163
200 201 202 203 210 211 212 213 216 220 221 222 223 224 225 228 249 250 251 252 280 281 282 283
310 311 312 319 320 321
407 407a
620 621 622 623 624 625 627 631 635
928 951
1403 1404

Safety suspect : adverse reaction possible

These additives vary greatly in the severity of the associated health concerns. In some cases, the jury is still out about their long-term safety. Other additives in this category are linked to severe effects in existing references. Refer to Additive Effects on page 109 for more info on each additive and the associated health concerns.

100 102 104 110 120 122 123 124 127 129 131 132 133 142 150 151 155 160b 172 173 174 175
200 201 202 203 210 211 212 213 216 218 220 221 222 223 224 225 228 235 249 250 251 252 264 280 281 282 283 290 296
310 311 312 319 320 321 337 338 349 355 385
405 407 407a 409 413 414 416 420 421 422 431 445 466 477 480 482 491
508 510 512 514 519 530 541 553 554 555 556 579
620 621 622 623 624 625 627 631 635 641
914 924 928 943a 943b 944 951 952 954 955 956 965 966 967
1201 1422 1520 1521

Not recommended for those with salicylate intolerance

102 104 110 120 122 123 124 127 132 133 142 150 151 155
211 212 213 216 218
310 311 312 321
621 623 627

Not recommended for those with kidney or liver problems

172 181
201 202 203 211 220 228 252 261
310 336 337 380 385
420 421 450 450a 451 452
508 510 511 514 518 519 554 555 556
622
914 951 952 954 955 956 1201 1520

Recently added to Australian standards

Little information about safety is available for these additives.

127 143 150 160d 160e 164 173 174 175
242
354 359 363 368
407a 431 445 472f
530 555 560 580 586
635 640 641
914 943a 943b 944 946 953 955 956 957 961 965 966 967 968
1001 1521

Appendix 2: Consumer information lines

COMPANY	PHONE		COMPANY	PHONE
Arnott's	1800242492		Maggi	1800025361
Birds Eye	1800061270		Masterfoods	1800816016
CC's Corn Chips	1800501441		Mainland	1800032479
Campbells	1800663366		Meadow Lea	1800638112
Cerebos Foods	1800656115		Mills and Wares	(08)93373222
Coles	1800061562		Miracle	1800677807
Continental	1800888997		Nannas	1800061279
Copperpot Dips	(08)82817710		Nestle	1800025361
Cottees	1800244054		Olive Grove	1800638112
Crisco Oils	1800638112		Olivio Bertolli	1800628400
Devondale	1800032479		Pampas	1800628883
Dolmio	1800816016		Pauls	1800676961
Dorata	1800688771		Tandaco	1800656115
Doritos	1800025789		Safcol	1800819785
Farmland	1800061562		Sanitarium	1800673392
Flora	1800628400		Sara Lee	1800650056
Four and Twenty	1800061279		Sea Lord	1800061279
Gold n Canola	1800638112		Signature Range	1800880078
Greens	1800803605		Smiths	1800025789
Heinz Watties	1800037058		SPC	1800805168
Herbert Adams	1800061279		Streets	1800643336
I&J	1800061279		Taings	1800682464
John West	1800888119		Westons	1800643287
Kellogg's	1800000474		White Wings	1800025768
Kettle Chips	1800806128		Woolworths WA	(08)93515222
Kraft	1800033275			
Lean Cuisines	1800025361			
Lowan	1800355718			
McCain	1800065521			

Appendix 3: Useful contacts

Additive Alert: Your Guide to Safer Shopping

www.additivealert.com.au

We welcome comments and feedback for future editions from consumers and manufacturers alike. Please feel free to e-mail us at additivealert@bigpond.com

Food Standards Australia New Zealand

www.foodstandards.gov.au

This is the regulatory body in Australia and New Zealand that controls the use of food additives in our food as per the *Food Standards Code*.

PO Box 7186
Canberra ACT 2610

Phone: (02) 6271 2222
Fax: (02) 6271 2278

E-mail: Information Officer:
         info@foodstandards.gov.au

Food Intolerance Network

www.fedup.com.au

This is a NSW-based organisation providing support and assistance for people with food-intolerance issues. This is an excellent and well-maintained information site with a wealth of detail about the effects of food additives on both adults and children. It also provides scientific references in relation to the effects of many food additives. You can subscribe to the free *Failsafe* newsletter, which highlights current issues, research, product updates, recipes and support forums around the country.

E-mail: sdengate@ozemail.com.au

Campaign for Truth in Medicine

www.campaignfortruth.com

This is a UK-based organisation committed to the distribution of accurate health and treatment information from properly researched sources that lead citizens to informed choices. Free monthly newsletter is available about toxins and chemicals in food, personal care and household products. They also have a good online selection of books about a variety of associated topics, especially avoiding toxins and chemicals in daily life.

Campaign for Truth In Labelling

www.truthinlabeling.org

This is a US-based organisation dedicated to the full disclosure of the presence of MSG in all its forms in all foods and personal-care products. They have lots of interesting information and research articles about the effects of MSG and it's unlabelled cohorts such as hydrolysed vegetable protein.

Diabetes Australia

www.diabetesaustralia.com.au

This is a not-for-profit organisation dedicated to minimising the impact of diabetes on Australian society. They are involved in education and awareness strategies and the development of national policies to combat the rising incidence of the disease. This is an excellent resource site for those with diabetes or anyone interested in learning more about the disease, its management and prevention.

Centre for Science in the Public Interest
www.cspinet.org

This US-based nutrition advocacy group has an interesting website that covers a wide range of issues relating to food safety, regulation and labelling in the US. They also publish an award winning newsletter called *Nutrition Action Health Letter* that you can subscribe to and view back copies of online.

Holistic Healing Web Page
www.holisticmed.com

This is a wide-ranging site containing a wealth of information about health, nutrition and wellbeing issues.

Sucralose Toxicity Information Centre
www.holisticmed.com/splenda/

This site presents facts about the artificial sweetener Splenda.

Aspartame (Nutrasweet) Toxicity Information Centre
http://www.holisticmed.com/aspartame/

This site provides detailed scientific and general documents relating to the toxicity of Nutrasweet, Equal, Diet Coke and other Aspartame containing items.

Asthma Foundations
www.asthmaaustralia.org.au

Freecall 1800 645 130 to enquire about support services and resources in your area.

Australian Breastfeeding Association
www.breastfeeding.asn.au

The Australian Breastfeeding Association is an organisation of people interested in the promotion and maintenance of breastfeeding.

Dr Peter Dingle
www.drdingle.com

Website for Dr Peter Dingle. Has some information about additives and links to the *Positive Living Foundation*. Lots of interesting information about avoiding toxins in your diet and environment and general resources for healthy living.

Dr Igor Tabrizian
www.nutritionreviewservice.com.au

Website for Dr Igor Tabrizian, a Perth based specialist in the nutritional basis of disease. A wealth of information on this site and especially valuable for those with an interest in autism or cancer prevention and treatment. Author of 6 books on Nutritional Medicine. Dr Tabrizian also trains medical practitioners in the application of Diagnostic Orthomolecular Medicine. Contact NRS to find out more about Dr Tabrizian's lecture series, books, CDs and DVDs, professional training or to locate a DOM trained practitioner in your area.

Dr Joseph Mercola
www.mercola.com

Homepage for US-based Dr Joseph Mercola, author of the Total Health Program. Subscribe for his weekly newsletter which contains up-to-date comment on health issues and a great reference site for all health-related questions.

The Parents' Jury
www.parentsjury.com.au

The parents' jury is a web-based network of parents who wish to improve the food and physical activity environments for children in Australia. The Parents' Jury is a forum for parents to voice their views on children's food and physical activity issues, and to collectively advocate for the improvement of children's food and physical activity environments (for example, reduced marketing targeted at young children, more healthy choices for school canteens, and making neighbourhoods safer and more child friendly). Subscribe for their regular newsletter to keep up to date with issues relating to childhood obesity and diabetes.

Appendix 4: Additive effects

#	NAME	ADVERSE REACTION
100–199		
100	Curcumin or Turmeric	Derived from the Turmeric plant root but not the same thing as the common spice Turmeric – can also be produced artificially. Generally regarded as safe for use in foods, but some sources list concerns over long-term safety. Regard with caution – occasional use recommended as safe.
101	Riboflavin or riboflavin 5'-phosphate sodium	
102	Tartrazine	Linked to hyperactivity, skin rashes, migraines, behavioural problems, thyroid problems, and chromosome damage. Banned in Norway and Austria.
103	Alkanet or Alkannin	Linked to hyperactivity.
104	Quinoline yellow	Linked to hyperactivity, skin rashes, asthmatics should avoid. Banned in USA and Norway - previously banned in Australia.
110	Sunset yellow FCF	Suspected carcinogen, allergies, hyperactivity, upset stomach, skin rashes, kidney tumours, and chromosomal damage. Banned in Norway.
120	Carmines or Carminic acid or Cochineal	Red dye derived from a beetle. Commonly linked to hyperactivity, some studies suggest possibly toxic to embryo.
122	Azorubine or Carmoisine	Suspected carcinogen, mutagen, skin rashes, oedema, and hyperactivity. Banned in Sweden, USA, Austria and Norway.
123	Amaranth	Suspected carcinogen, mutagen, linked to hyperactivity, asthma and eczema. Banned in USA (1976), Russia, Austria, Norway and others.
124	Ponceau 4R	Suspected carcinogen, linked to hyperactivity and asthma. Banned in USA and Norway.
127	Erythrosine	Suspected carcinogen, linked to thyroid abnormality, brain dysfunction, hyperactivity, and light sensitivity. Banned in Norway.

#	NAME	ADVERSE REACTION
129	Allura Red AC	Suspected carcinogen, skin rashes, hypersensitivity. Banned in Denmark, Belgium, France, Germany, Switzerland, Austria, and Norway.
132	Indigotine	Suspected carcinogen, linked to hyperactivity, nausea, breathing difficulty, skin reactions, blood pressure. Banned in Norway.
133	Brilliant Blue	Suspected carcinogen, linked to hyperactivity, asthmatics should avoid. Banned in Belgium, France, Germany, Switzerland, Sweden, Austria, and Norway.
140	Chlorophyll	
141	Chlorophyll-copper complex	
142	Green S	Hypersensitivity, allergic reactions, asthmatics should avoid. Banned in USA, Sweden, Norway, UK..
143	Fast Green FCF	Can cause bladder tumours.
150	Caramel	Linked to gastro intestinal problems, hypersensitivity. Safety suspect. 150(i) seems safest.
150a	Caramel i (Plain Caramel)	Linked to gastro intestinal problems, hypersensitivity. Safety suspect. 150(i) seems safest.
150b	Caramel ii (Caustic Sulphite Caramel)	Linked to gastro intestinal problems, hypersensitivity. Safety suspect. 150(i) seems safest.
150c	Caramel iii (Ammonia Caramel)	Linked to gastro intestinal problems, hypersensitivity. Safety suspect. 150(i) seems safest.
150d	Caramel iv (Sulphite Ammonia Caramel)	Linked to gastro intestinal problems, hypersensitivity. Safety suspect. 150(i) seems safest.
151	Brilliant Black BN or Brilliant Black PN	Linked to bowel disorders, hyperactivity, asthmatics should avoid. Banned in US, Denmark, France, Germany, Switzerland, Sweden, Austria, Norway.
153	Carbon Black or vegetable carbon	Suspected carcinogen. Banned in US.
155	Brown HT	Suspected carcinogen and mutagen. Linked to asthma, skin irritation. Banned in US, Denmark, France, Germany, Switzerland, Sweden, Austria, Norway, Belgium.

#	NAME	ADVERSE REACTION
160a	Carotene	
160b	Annatto extracts	Hypersensitivity, allergic reactions, skin irritations, linked to behaviour and learning problems. Concerns about toxicity still being evaluated by JECFA yet is still freely used.
160c	Paprika oleoresins	Little info available.
160d	Lycopene	
160e	b-apo-8' carotenal	
160f	b-apo-8' carotenoic acid or methyl ethyl ester	
161a	Flavoxanthin	
161b	Lutein	
161c	Kryptoxanthin	
161d	Rubixanthin	
161e	Violoxanthin	
161f	Rhodoxanthin	
161g	Xanthophylls (Canthaxanthin)	
162	Beet red	Considered safe for use in foods and a much better option than coal tar dyes. Avoid for very young children and infants due to high sodium nitrate content.
163	Anthocyanins or grape skin extract or blackcurrant extract	Asthmatics should avoid.
164	Saffron or crocetin or crocin	
170	Calcium Carbonate	
171	Titanium Dioxide	Commonly used now in white foods such as vanilla ice cream. Some concern over long-term safety in relation to reproduction and cancer. Regard with caution. Not recommended for regular consumption.
172	Iron oxide	Possible kidney damage. Suspected neurotoxin. Blindness in dog studies.
173	Aluminium	New to standards, previously not permitted in Australia. Banned in other countries.
174	Silver	New to standards, previously not permitted in Australia. Banned in other countries.
175	Gold	New to standards, previously not permitted in Australia. Banned in other countries.

#	NAME	ADVERSE REACTION
181	Tannic Acid or tannins	Large doses associated with gastric problems, kidney and liver damage.
200–299		
200	Sorbic acid	Skin irritant, behavioural problems. Asthmatics should avoid.
201	Sodium sorbate	Behavioural problems. Linked to asthma and kidney / liver problems.
202	Potassium sorbate	Possible liver damage, behavioural problems. Linked to asthma. Avoid if kidney or heart problems.
203	Calcium sorbate	Behavioural problems. Linked to Asthma and allergic reactions.
210	Benzoic acid	Hyperactivity, asthmatics should avoid, possible neurological dysfunctions.
211	Sodium benzoate	Hyperactivity, asthmatics should avoid, nettle rash, behavioural problems.
212	Potassium benzoate	Asthmatics should avoid, nettle rash, behavioural problems.
213	Calcium benzoate	Asthmatics should avoid, nettle rash, behavioural problems.
216	Propylparaben or propyl -p-hydroxy-benzoate	Asthmatics should avoid, contact dermatitis, eczema, mouth numbing.
218	Methylparaben or methyl-p-hydroxy-benzoate	Allergic reactions possible - skin and mouth.
220	Sulphur dioxide	Asthmatics should avoid, gastric irritation / damage, hyperactivity, behavioural problems, poss mutagen. Can be fatal to asthmatics.
221	Sodium sulphite	Asthmatics should avoid, gastric irritation, nausea, nettle rash and swelling, behavioural problems.
222	Sodium bisulphite	Asthmatics should avoid, gastric irritation, nausea, nettle rash and swelling, behavioural problems.
223	Sodium metabisulphite	Asthmatics should avoid, gastric irritation, nausea, nettle rash and swelling, behavioural problems.
224	Potassium metabisulphite	Asthmatics should avoid, gastric irritation, nausea, nettle rash and swelling, behavioural problems.
225	Potassium sulphite	Asthmatics should avoid, gastric irritation, nausea, nettle rash and swelling, behavioural problems.

#	NAME	ADVERSE REACTION
228	Potassium bisulphite	Asthmatics should avoid, gastric irritation, nausea, nettle rash and swelling, behavioural problems.
234	Nisin	
235	Natamycin or pimaricin	Can cause nausea, vomiting, diarrhoea and skin irritation.
242	Dimethyl dicarbonate	
249	Potassium nitrite	Behavioural problems, asthma, breathing difficulties, headaches, dizziness, possible carcinogen. Prohibited in foods for infants and young children.
250	Sodium nitrite	Hyperactivity, behavioural problems, asthma, headaches, dizziness, possible carcinogen. Prohibited in foods for infants and young children.
251	Sodium nitrate	Hyperactivity, behavioural problems, asthma, headaches, dizziness, possible carcinogen. Prohibited in foods for infants and young children.
252	Potassium nitrate	Hyperactivity, behavioural problems, asthma, headaches, dizziness, possible carcinogen, kidney inflammation. Prohibited in foods for infants and young children.
260	Acetic acid,glacial	
261	Potassium acetate or potassium diacetate	Those with kidney or liver problems should avoid.
262	Sodium acetates	
263	Calcium acetate	
264	Ammonium acetate	Nausea, vomiting, concerns about carcinogenicity. Avoid where possible, especially for children.
270	Lactic acid	Safe in foods but avoid for very young babies as may be unable to metabolise.
280	Propionic acid	Behavioural and learning problems, headaches. Asthma.
281	Sodium propionate	Behavioural and learning problems, headaches. Asthma.
282	Calcium propionate	Behavioural and learning problems, skin irritation, headaches, migraine. Asthma.
283	Potassium propionate	Behavioural and learning problems, migraine, headaches. Asthma.
290	Carbon dioxide	Reproductive and neurotoxicity, teratogen, possible links to infertility, on NIH hazards list.
296	Malic acid	Safe in foods but avoid for very young babies. Some reports of allergic reactions in sensitive people.

#	NAME	ADVERSE REACTION
297	Fumaric acid	

300–399

#	NAME	ADVERSE REACTION
300	Ascorbic acid	
301	Sodium ascorbate	
302	Calcium ascorbate	Those susceptible to kidney stones should avoid; otherwise regarded as safe.
303	Potassium ascorbate	
304	Ascorbyl palmitate	
306	Tocopherols concentrate, mixed	
307	a-Tocopherol	
308	g-Tocopheral	
309	d-Tocopheral	
310	Propyl gallate	Suspected carcinogen, asthmatics and aspirin sensitive people should avoid, liver damage, skin irritations. Prohibited in food for infants and young children as linked to blood disorder.
311	Octyl gallate	Asthmatics and aspirin sensitive people should avoid, gastric and skin irritations. Prohibited in foods for infants and young children.
312	Dodecyl gallate	Asthmatics and aspirin sensitive people should avoid, gastric and skin irritations. Prohibited in foods for infants and young children - caused deaths in animal tests.
315	Erythorbic acid	
316	Sodium erythorbate	Headaches reported by some sensitive people. Generally regarded as safe in foods.
319	Tert-butylhydroquinone	Linked to cancer, birth defects and can cause nausea, vomiting, delirium, collapse, and dermatitis. Dose of 5g is fatal - avoid it.
320	Butylated hydroxyanisole	Serious concerns about carcinogenic and estrogenic effects, asthmatics and aspirin sensitive people should avoid, causes metabolic changes and accumulates in body fat. Banned in Japan in 1958 -Not permitted in foods for infants and young children.
321	Butylated hydroxytoluene	Suspected carcinogen, asthmatics and aspirin sensitive people should avoid, skin irritation. Prohibited in foods for infants and young children.
322	Lecithin	

#	NAME	ADVERSE REACTION
325	Sodium lactate	
326	Potassium lactate	
327	Calcium lactate	
328	Ammonium lactate	
329	Magnesium lactate	
330	Citric acid	
331	Sodium citrates	
332	Potassium citrates	
333	Calcium citrates	
334	Tartaric acid	
335	Sodium tartrates	
336	Potassium tartrate	Those with kidney impairment should avoid.
337	Potassium sodium tartrate	Those with kidney impairment should avoid. Not recommended for those with heart problems or high blood pressure.
338	Phosphoric acid	Neurotoxicity, eye and skin irritant, large doses can lead to acidosis and hypocalcaemia.
339	Sodium phosphates	
340	Potassium phosphates	
341	Calcium phosphates	
342	Ammonium phosphates	New to standards.
343	Magnesium phosphates	
349	Ammonium malate	Unsuitable for infants and young children, skin irritations.
350	Sodium malates	
351	Potassium malates	
352	Calcium malates	
353	Metatartaric acid	
354	Calcium tartrate	New to standards.
355	Adipic acid	Severe eye irritant, toxic effect in rat studies including death - avoid it.
357	Potassium adipate	
359	Ammonium adipates	New to standards.
363	Succinic acid	New to standards.
365	Sodium fumarate	
366	Potassium fumarate	
367	Calcium fumarate	
368	Ammonium fumarate	New to standards.
380	Ammonium citrate or triammonium citrate	May interfere with liver and pancreas function - more study needed.
381	Ferric ammonium citrate	
385	Calcium disodium EDTA	Muscle cramps, kidney damage, gastrointestinal problems, banned in some countries.

#	NAME	ADVERSE REACTION
400–499		
400	Alginic acid	
401	Sodium alginate	
402	Potassium alginate	
403	Ammonium alginate	
404	Calcium alginate	
405	Propylene glycol alginate	Allergic reactions common, avoid in pregnancy - more study required.
406	Agar	
407	Carrageenan	Suspected carcinogen, linked to ulcerative colitis, damage to the immune system and concern about excitotoxic effects. Not recommended for children – more work needed. Many reports of IBS like symptoms associated with its regular use. Not recommended for regular consumption.
407a	Processed eucheuma seaweed	As above – some studies show that undegraded carrageenan can be broken down into degraded carrageenan in the gut. Regard with caution – occasional use only suggested.
409	Arabinogalactan or larch gum	Allergic reactions, possible weak carcinogen - more work required.
410	Locust bean gum	Large amounts may cause abdominal pain, diarrhoea.
412	Guar gum	
413	Tragacanth gum	Asthma, skin rashes, gastrointestinal upsets, contact dermatitis.
414	Acacia or gum Arabic	Asthma, skin rashes in sensitive people.
415	Xanthan gum	
416	Karaya gum	Asthma. Urticaria, gastrointestinal upsets, dermatitis.
418	Gellan gum	
420	Sorbitol or sorbitol syrup	Not suitable for diabetics, infants and young children, liver toxicity, gastrointestinal upsets. Prohibited in foods for infants and young children.
421	Mannitol	Not for diabetics, infants and young children, or those with kidney / liver impairment. Linked to hyperactivity, kidney damage. On NIH Hazards list.
422	Glycerin or glycerol	Headaches, high blood sugar levels, eye skin irritation in sensitive people.

#	NAME	ADVERSE REACTION
431	Polyethylene (40) stearate	Suspected carcinogen, skin allergies - new to standard.
432	Polysorbate 20 or polyoxyethylene sorbitan monolaurate	Suspected carcinogen - more work needed.
433	Polysorbate 80 or polyoxyethylene (20) sorbitan monooleate	Suspected carcinogen - more work needed.
435	Polysorbate 60	Suspected carcinogen - more testing needed.
436	Polysorbate 65	Suspected carcinogen - more testing needed.
440	Pectins	
440a	Pectins	
440b	Pectins	
441	Gelatine	
442	Ammonium salts of phosphatidic acid	
444	Sucrose acetate isobutyrate	
445	Gylcerol esters of wood rosins	Headaches, high blood sugar levels, eye skin irritation in sensitive people.
450	Potassium pyrophosphate	Linked to kidney stones in susceptible people, otherwise regarded as safe.
451	Potassium tripolyphosphate	Linked to kidney stones in susceptible people, otherwise regarded as safe.
452	Potassium polymetaphosphate	Linked to kidney stones in susceptible people, otherwise regarded as safe.
460	Cellulose microcrystalline and powdered	Most sources regard as safe although banned in UK in baby food only.
461	Methyl cellulose	
463	Hydroxypropyl cellulose	
464	Hydroxypropyl methylcellulose	
465	Methyl ethyl cellulose	Flatulence, intestinal upsets, diarrhoea.
466	Sodium carboxymethylcellulose	Suspected carcinogen, flatulence, intestinal discomfort and diarrhoea.
469	Sodium caseinate	Previously permitted in Australia, but no longer included in standards.
470	Aluminuim, calcium, sodium, magnesium, potassium and ammonium salts of fatty acids.	
471	Mono and di glycerides of fatty acids	
472a	Acetic and fatty acid esters of glycerol	

#	NAME	ADVERSE REACTION
472b	Lactic and fatty acid esters of glycerol	
472c	Citric and fatty acid esters of glycerol	
472e	Diacetyltartaric and fatty acid esters of glycerol	Headaches, high blood sugar levels, eye skin irritation in sensitive people. JECFA still evaluating.
472f	Mixed tartaric acetic and fatty acid esters of glycerol	
473	Sucrose esters of fatty acids	
475	Polyglycerol esters of fatty acids	
476	Polyglycerol esters of interesterified ricinoleic acid	
477	Propylene glycol mono and di-esters	Derived from propylene glycol.
480	Dioctyl sodium sulphosuccinate	More testing being done especially in relation to children and infants.
481	Sodium lactylate	
482	Calcium lactylate	Adverse reactions have occurred in animal tests.
491	Sorbitan monostearate	Some adverse effects recorded in animal studies in large doses – growth retardation. Considered safe in foods in low doses – more studies needed.
492	Sorbitan tristearate	Some adverse effects recorded in animal studies in large doses – growth retardation. Considered safe in foods in low doses – more studies needed.

500–599

#	NAME	ADVERSE REACTION
500	Sodium carbonate or bi carbonate	Regarded as safe in small amounts.
501	Potassium carbonates	
503	Ammonium bicarbonate or ammonium hydrogen carbonate	Can irritate mucous membranes and lead to skin and scalp irritations in some people.
504	Magnesium carbonate	
507	Hydrochloric acid	Stomach and mouth irritant - some sources list as possible teratogenic.
508	Potassium chloride	Associated with gastric ulcers, circulatory collapse, nausea, and liver toxicity. Not recommended for children.

#	NAME	ADVERSE REACTION
509	Calcium chloride	Stomach irritant in sensitive people.
510	Ammonium chloride	Large amounts can cause acidosis - nausea, headaches, and insomnia. Those with kidney / liver problems should avoid.
511	Magnesium chloride	Caused kidney damage in dogs so those with kidney damage may wish to avoid.
512	Stannous chloride	Nausea, headache, gastric upset. Skin and mucous membrane irritant.
514	Sodium sulphate	Unsuitable for infants and children and those with kidney /liver problems due to high sodium content - Skin irritant.
515	Potassium sulphate	Regarded as safe in small doses.
516	Calcium sulphate	
518	Magnesium sulphate	Laxative effect, low blood pressure, drowsiness, those with kidney damage should avoid.
519	Cupric sulphate	Linked to gastrointestinal problems, those with kidney / liver problems should avoid, neurotoxicity.
526	Calcium hydroxide	
529	Calcium oxide	
530	Magnesium oxide	Caused tumours in hamsters - can cause diarrhoea.
535	Sodium ferrocyanide	
536	Potassium ferrocyanide	
541	Sodium aluminium phosphate	Thought to release aluminium during digestion - concerns about skeletal abnormalities, dementia, and Parkinson's type illness.
542	Bone phosphate	
551	Silicon dioxide	
552	Calcium silicate	
553	Magnesium silicate or talc	Linked to stomach and ovarian cancers. Respiratory problems.
554	Sodium aluminosilicate	Linked to Alzheimer's and nerve damage, bone diseases, kidney damage, and neurotoxicity.
555	Potassium aluminium silicate	Linked to Alzheimer's and nerve damage, bone diseases, kidney damage, and neurotoxicity.
556	Calcium aluminium silicate	Linked to Alzheimer's and nerve damage, bone diseases, kidney damage, and neurotoxicity.
558	Bentonite	
559	Aluminium silicate	

#	NAME	ADVERSE REACTION
560	Potassium silicate	Little info available.
570	Stearic acid or fatty acid	Can cause allergic reactions in sensitive people - skin irritant.
575	Glucono d-lactone or glucono delta lactone	
577	Potassium gluconate	
578	Calcium gluconate	
579	Ferrous gluconate	Diarrhoea, vomiting, gastrointestinal upsets. Research showed it caused tumours in mice. Regard with caution.
580	Magnesium gluconate	New to standards - no info avail - regard with caution.
586	4-Hexylresorcinol	New to standards - no info avail - regard with caution.

600–899

#	NAME	ADVERSE REACTION
620	L-Glutamic acid	Unsuitable for infants and children, allergic and hypersensitive reactions, headaches, nausea, sleeplessness.
621	Monosodium L-glutamate or MSG	Asthma, hyperactivity, depression, mood changes, sleeplessness, nausea, migraine, linked to infertility, teratogen, convulsions, abdominal discomfort. See text re other hidden sources of MSG.
622	Monopotassium L-glutamate	Problems in people with poor kidney function, headache, asthma, nausea, restlessness.
623	Calcium glutamate	Asthmatics and aspirin sensitive people should avoid.
624	Monoammonium L-glutamate	Varied allergic reactions in some people. Not recommended for asthmatics.
625	Magnesium glutamate	Varied allergic reactions in some people. Not recommended for asthmatics.
627	Disodium 5'-guanylate	Asthmatics and aspirin sensitive people should avoid, linked to hyperactivity, gout sufferers avoid. Prohibited in foods for infants and young children.
631	Disodium 5'-inosinate	May trigger gout symptoms, varied reactions reported. Prohibited in foods for infants and young children. Not recommended for asthmatics.

#	NAME	ADVERSE REACTION
635	Disodium 5'-ribonucleotides	Can cause terrible itchy skin rashes, hyperactivity, sleeplessness, mood changes, many varied ill effects reported. Banned in some other countries -very common in Aust foods. Asthmatics should avoid.
636	Maltol	More work needed – regard with caution.
637	Ethyl maltol	Some concerns about toxicity- more work required.
640	Glycine	Some concerns about long-term safety – more study needed as use becomes more widespread.
641	L-Leucine	Caused birth defects in laboratory animals - more testing needed - Regard with caution.

900–1099

#	NAME	ADVERSE REACTION
900a	Polydimethylsiloxane or dimethylpolysiloxane	Suspected carcinogen. Can contain formaldehyde.
901	Beeswax white and yellow	Occasionally causes allergic reactions in sensitive people.
903	Carnauba wax	Rare skin allergy reported in sensitive people.
904	Shellac	Rare skin allergy in sensitive people
905b	Petrolatum or Petroleum jelly	Can inhibit absorption of digestive fats, allergic skin reactions possible in some people.
914	Oxidised polyethylene	Linked to cancer, kidney and liver damage. Used as a protective coating on fruits, nuts and vegetables.
920	L-Cysteine monohydrochloride	Derived from human hair – commonly used in bread products.
941	Nitrogen	
942	Nitrous oxide	
943a	Butane	Caused cancer in animal tests, neurotoxicity, on NIH Hazards list. Petroleum derivative - avoid it.
943b	Isobutane	Neurotoxic at high concentrations; on NIH hazards list.
944	Propane	Neurotoxic at high concentrations; on NIH hazards list.
946	Octafluorocyclobutane	More info needed - regard with caution.
950	Acesulphame potassium	Caused cancer and tumours in animal tests.

#	NAME	ADVERSE REACTION
951	Aspartame	Linked to many health problems including cancer, asthma, nausea, depressions, hyperactivity, and seizures. The most complained about food additive accounting for 75% of all complaints to FDA.
952	Calcium cyclamate or sodium cyclamate	Suspected carcinogen, animal tests caused testicular damage and embryo damage in rats. Banned in UK and USA in 1970 but still permitted in Australia.
953	Isomalt	
954	Saccharin or calcium / sodium / potassium saccharin	Known carcinogen especially linked to bladder and reproductive cancers. Banned in US in 1977 but reinstated with strict labelling provisions.
955	Sucralose	Linked to neurological and immunological disorders, caused kidney and liver damage in tests. More research needed - avoid it.
956	Alitame	Liver abnormalities in lab tests - more research needed.
957	Thaumatin	Not for use in infants' foods. Little information available - regard with caution.
961	Neotame	Little info available – similar to aspartame so regard with caution.
965	Maltitol and maltitol syrup or hydrogenated glucose syrup	Caused increased incidence of tumours in animal tests.
966	Lactitol	Diarrhoea in high doses, more work needed.
967	Xylitol	Diarrhoea, stomach upsets, early studies showed carcinogenic potential. More recently regarded as safe in small doses. More work needed.
968	Erythritol	Little info available - regard with caution.

1100–		
1100	a-amylase	
1101	Proteases (papain, bromelain, ficin)	Little info available.
1102	Glucose oxidase	Little info available.
1104	Lipases	
1105	Lysozyme	
1200	Polydextrose	

#	NAME	ADVERSE REACTION
1201	Polyvinylpyrrolidone	Cancer, lung and kidney damage; liver toxicity, allergic reactions, skin reactions. Made from acetylene, hydrogen, formaldehyde, ammonia
1400	Dextrin roasted starch	Allergic reactions reported, celiacs should avoid
1401	Acid treated starch	Allergic reactions reported, celiacs should avoid
1402	Alkaline treated starch	Allergic reactions reported, celiacs should avoid
1403	Bleached starch	Linked to asthma as may be treated with sulphur dioxide
1404	Oxidised starch	Linked to asthma as may be treated with sulphur dioxide
1405	Enzyme treated starch	Allergic reactions reported, celiacs should avoid
1410	Monostarch phosphate	
1412	Distarch phosphate	
1413	Phosphated distarch phosphate	
1414	Acetylated distarch phosphate	
1420	Starch acetate esterified with acetic anhydride	Allergic reactions reported, celiacs should avoid
1422	Acetylated distarch adipate	Animal tests showed slowed growth rates and renal lesions. Common in baby foods.
1440	Hydroxypropyl starch	
1442	Hydroxypropyl distarch phosphate	
1450	Starch sodium octenylsuccinate	
1505	Triethyl citrate	
1518	Triacetin	
1520	Propylene glycol	Large doses can be toxic, kidney failure, depression of CNS, liver damage, teratogen, on NIH Hazards list. Humectant used to coat fruit and vegetables. USA has placed a total recall of any medication containing this additive yet still permitted in food.
1521	Polyethylene glycol 8000	Caused renal failure in some tests, more info needed, avoid it for now

Appendix 5: Food Additives Alphabetical Listing

PRESCRIBED NAME	NUMBER

Symbols used in this list:

a = alpha; *b* = beta; *d* = delta; *g* = gamma.

Prescribed Name	Code
Acacia or gum Arabic (thickener, stabiliser)	414
Acesulphame potassium (sweetener)	950
Acetic acid, glacial (acidity regulator)	260
Acetic and fatty acid esters of glycerol (emulsifier, stabiliser)	472a
Acetylated distarch adipate (thickener, stabiliser)	1422
Acetylated distarch phosphate (thickener, stabiliser)	1414
Acid treated starch (thickener, stabiliser)	1401
Adipic acid (acidity regulator)	355
Agar (thickener, gelling agent, stabiliser)	406
Alginic acid (thickener, stabiliser)	400
Alitame (sweetener)	956
Alkaline treated starch (thickener, stabiliser)	1402
Alkanet or Alkannin (colour)	103
Allura red AC (colour)	129
Aluminium (colour)	173
Aluminium, calcium, sodium, magnesium, potassium and ammonium salts of fatty acids (emulsifier, stabiliser, anti-caking agent)	470
Aluminium silicate	559
Amaranth (colour)	123

Ammonium acetate (acidity regulator)	264
Ammonium adipates (acidity regulator)	359
Ammonium alginate (thickener, stabiliser)	403
Ammonium bicarbonate or Ammonium hydrogen carbonate (acidity regulator, raising agent)	503
Ammonium chloride (bulking agent)	510
Ammonium citrate or triammonium citrate (acidity regulator)	380
Ammonium fumarate (acidity regulator)	368
Ammonium lactate (acidity regulator)	328
Ammonium malate (acidity regulator)	349
Ammonium phosphates (acidity regulator)	342
Ammonium salts of phosphatidic acid (emulsifier)	442
alpha - amylase (enzyme)	1100
Annatto extracts (colour)	160b
Anthocyanins or Grape skin extract or Blackcurrant extract (colour)	163
Arabinogalactan or Larch gum (thickener, gelling agent, stabiliser)	409
Ascorbic acid (antioxidant)	300
Ascorbyl palmitate (antioxidant)	304
Aspartame (sweetener)	951
Azorubine or Carmoisine (colour)	122
beta-apo-8' Carotenal (colour)	160e
beta-apo-8' Carotenoic acid methyl or ethyl ester (colour)	160f
Beeswax, white and yellow (glazing agent)	901
Beet red (colour)	162
Bentonite (anti-caking agent)	558
Benzoic acid (preservative)	210
Bleached starch (thickener, stabiliser)	1403
Bone phosphate (anti-caking agent, emulsifier)	542

Brilliant black BN or Brilliant black PN (colour)	151
Brilliant blue FCF (colour)	133
Brown HT (colour)	155
Butane (propellant)	943a
Butylated hydroxyanisole (antioxidant)	320
Butylated hydroxytoluene (antioxidant)	321
Calcium acetate (acidity regulator)	263
Calcium alginate (thickener, stabiliser, gelling agent)	404
Calcium aluminium silicate (anti-caking agent)	556
Calcium ascorbate (antioxidant)	302
Calcium benzoate (preservative)	213
Calcium carbonate (colour, anti-caking agent)	170
Calcium chloride (firming agent)	509
Calcium citrates (acidity regulator, stabiliser)	333
Calcium cyclamate or sodium cyclamate or cyclamate	952
Calcium disodium ethylenediaminetetraacetate or calcium disodium EDTA (preservative, antioxidant)	385
Calcium fumarate (acidity regulator)	367
Calcium gluconate (acidity regulator, firming agent)	578
Calcium glutamate (flavour enhancer)	623
Calcium hydroxide (acidity regulator, firming agent)	526
Calcium lactate (acidity regulator)	327
Calcium lactylate or Calcium oleyl lactylate or Calcium stearoyl lactylate (emulsifier, stabiliser)	482
Calcium malates (acidity regulator)	352
Calcium oxide (acidity regulator)	529
Calcium phosphates (acidity regulator, emulsifier, stabiliser, anti-caking agent)	341
Calcium propionate (preservative)	282
Calcium silicate (anti-caking agent)	552

Calcium sorbate (preservative)	203
Calcium sulphate (firming agent)	516
Calcium tartrate (acidity regulator)	354
Caramel I (colour)	150a
Caramel II (colour)	150b
Caramel III (colour)	150c
Caramel IV (colour)	150d
Carbon black or vegetable carbon (colour)	153
Carbon dioxide (propellant)	290
Carmines or Carminic acid or Cochineal (colour)	120
Carnauba wax (glazing agent)	903
Carotene (colour)	160a
Carrageenan (thickener, gelling agent, stabiliser)	407
Cellulose microcrystalline and powdered (anti-caking agent)	460
Chlorophyll (colour)	140
Chlorophyll-copper complex (colour)	141
Choline salts (emulsifier)	1001
Citric acid (acidity regulator, antioxidant)	330
Citric and fatty acid esters of glycerol (emulsifier, stabiliser)	472c
Cupric sulphate (mineral salt)	519
Curcumin or Turmeric (colour)	100
Dextrin roasted starch (thickener, stabiliser)	1400
Diacetyltartaric and fatty acid esters of glycerol (emulsifier)	472e
Dimethyl dicarbonate (preservative)	242
Dioctyl sodium sulphosuccinate (emulsifier)	480
Disodium 5 -guanylate (flavour enhancer)	627
Disodium 5 -inosinate (flavour enhancer)	631
Disodium 5'-ribonucleotides (flavour enhancer)	635
Distarch phosphate (thickener, stabiliser)	1412

Dodecyl gallate (antioxidant)	312
Enzyme treated starches (thickener, stabiliser)	1405
Erythorbic acid (antioxidant)	315
Erythritol (humectant, sweetener)	968
Erythrosine (colour)	127
Ethyl maltol (flavour enhancer)	637
Fast green FCF (colour)	143
Ferric ammonium citrate (acidity regulator, anti-caking agent)	381
Ferrous gluconate (colour retention agent)	579
Flavoxanthin (colour)	161a
Fumaric acid (acidity regulator)	297
Gellan gum (thickener, stabiliser, gelling agent)	418
Glucono *delta* -lactone or Glucono delta-lactone (acidity	575
Glucose oxidase (antioxidant)	1102
Glycerin or glycerol (humectant)	422
Glycerol esters of wood rosins (emulsifier, stabiliser)	445
Glycine (flavour enhancer)	640
Gold (colour)	175
Green S (colour)	142
Guar gum (thickener, stabiliser)	412
4-Hexylresorcinol (antioxidant)	586
Hydrochloric acid (acidity regulator)	507
Hydroxypropyl cellulose (thickener, stabiliser, emulsifier)	463
Hydroxypropyl distarch phosphate (thickener, stabiliser)	1442
Hydroxypropyl methylcellulose (thickener, stabiliser, emulsifier)	464
Hydroxypropyl starch (thickener, stabiliser)	1440
Indigotine (colour)	132
Iron oxide (colour)	172

Isobutane (propellant)	943b
Isomalt (humectant, sweetener, bulking agent, anti-caking agent)	953
Karaya gum (thickener, stabiliser)	416
Kryptoxanthin (colour)	161c
Lactic acid (acidity regulator)	270
Lactic and fatty acid esters of glycerol (emulsifier, stabiliser)	472b
Lactitol (sweetener, humectant)	966
L-Cysteine monohydrochloride (raising agent)	920
Lecithin (antioxidant, emulsifier)	322
L-Glutamic acid (flavour enhancer)	620
Lipases (enzyme)	1104
L-Leucine (flavour enhancer)	641
Locust bean gum or Carob bean gum (thickener, stabiliser)	410
Lutein (colour)	161b
Lycopene (colour)	160d
Lysozyme (enzyme, preservative)	1105
Magnesium carbonate (acidity regulator, anti-caking agent)	504
Magnesium chloride (firming agent)	511
Magnesium gluconate (acidity regulatory, firming agent)	580
Magnesium glutamate (flavour enhancer)	625
Magnesium lactate (acidity regulator)	329
Magnesium oxide (anti-caking agent)	530
Magnesium phosphates (acidity regulator, anti-caking agent)	343
Magnesium silicate or Talc (anti-caking agent)	553
Magnesium sulphate (firming agent)	518
Malic acid (acidity regulator)	296
Maltitol and maltitol syrup or hydrogenated glucose syrup (sweetener, stabiliser, emulsifier, humectant)	965

Maltol (flavour enhancer)	636
Mannitol (sweetener, humectant)	421
Metatartaric acid (acidity regulator)	353
Methyl ethyl cellulose (thickener, stabiliser, emulsifier, foaming agent)	465
Methyl cellulose (thickener, stabiliser, emulsifier)	461
Methylparaben or Methyl-p-hydroxy-benzoate (preservative)	218
Mixed tartaric, acetic and fatty acid esters of glycerol (emulsifier, stabiliser)	472f
Mono- and di-glycerides of fatty acids (emulsifier, stabiliser)	471
Monoammonium L-glutamate (flavour enhancer)	624
Monopotassium L-glutamate (flavour enhancer)	622
Monosodium L-glutamate or MSG (flavour enhancer)	621
Monostarch phosphate (thickener, stabiliser)	1410
Natamycin or Pimaricin (preservative)	235
Neotame (sweetener)	961
Nisin (preservative)	234
Nitrogen (propellant)	941
Nitrous oxide (propellant)	942
Octafluorocyclobutane (propellant)	946
Octyl gallate (antioxidant)	311
Oxidised polyethylene (humectant)	914
Oxidised starch (thickener, stabiliser)	1404
Paprika oleoresins (colour)	160c
Pectins (thickener, stabiliser, gelling agent)	440
Petrolatum or petroleum jelly (glazing agent)	905b
Phosphated distarch phosphate (thickener, stabiliser)	1413
Phosphoric acid (acidity regulator)	338
Polydextrose (humectant, bulking agent, stabiliser, thickener)	1200

Polydimethylsiloxane or Dimethylpolysiloxane (anti-caking agent, emulsifier)	900a
Polyethylene (40) stearate (emulsifier)	431
Polyethylene glycol 8000 (antifoaming agent)	1521
Polyglycerol esters of fatty acids (emulsifier)	475
Polyglycerol esters of interesterified ricinoleic acid (emulsifier)	476
Polysorbate 60 or Polyoxyethylene (20) sorbitan monostearate (emulsifier)	435
Polysorbate 65 or Polyoxyethylene (20) sorbitan tristearate (emulsifier)	436
Polysorbate 80 or Polyoxyethylene (20) sorbitan monooleate (emulsifier)	433
Polyvinylpyrrolidone (stabiliser)	1201
Ponceau 4R (colour)	124
Potassium acetate or Potassium diacetate (acidity regulator)	261
Potassium adipate (acidity regulator)	357
Potassium alginate (thickener, stabiliser)	402
Potassium aluminium silicate	555
Potassium ascorbate (antioxidant)	303
Potassium benzoate (preservative)	212
Potassium bisulphite (preservative)	228
Potassium carbonates (acidity regulator, stabiliser)	501
Potassium chloride (gelling agent)	508
Potassium citrates (acidity regulator, stabiliser)	332
Potassium ferrocyanide (anti-caking agent)	536
Potassium fumarate (acidity regulator)	366
Potassium gluconate (sequestrant)	577
Potassium lactate (acidity regulator, humectant, bulking agent)	326
Potassium malates (acidity regulator)	351
Potassium metabisulphite (preservative)	224

Potassium nitrate (preservative, colour fixative)	252
Potassium nitrite (preservative, colour fixative)	249
Potassium phosphates (acidity regulator, emulsifier, stabiliser)	340
Potassium polymetaphosphate or Sodium metaphosphate, insoluble or Sodium polyphosphates, glassy (emulsifier, stabiliser)	452
Potassium propionate (preservative)	283
Potassium pyrophosphate or Sodium acid pyrophosphate or Sodium pyrophosphate (emulsifiers, acidity regulators, stabilisers)	450
Potassium silicate (anti-caking agent)	560
Potassium sodium tartrate (acidity regulator, stabiliser)	337
Potassium sorbate (preservative)	202
Potassium sulphate (acidity regulator)	515
Potassium sulphite (preservative)	225
Potassium tartrate or Potassium acid tartrate (acidity regulator, stabiliser)	336
Potassium tripolyphosphate or Sodium tripolyphosphate (acidity regulator)	451
Processed eucheuma seaweed (thickener, gelling agent, stabiliser)	407a
Propane (propellant)	944
Propionic acid (preservative)	280
Propyl gallate (antioxidant)	310
Propylene glycol (humectant)	1520
Propylene glycol alginate (thickener, emulsifier)	405
Propylene glycol mono- and di-esters or Propylene glycol esters of fatty acids (emulsifier)	477
Propylparaben or Propyl-p-hydroxy-benzoate (preservative)	216
Proteases (papain, bromelain, ficin) (stabiliser, enzyme)	1101
Quinoline yellow (colour)	104
Rhodoxanthin (colour)	161f
Riboflavin or Riboflavin 5'-phosphate sodium (colour)	101

Rubixanthin (colour)	161d
Saccharin or calcium saccharin or sodium saccharine or potassium saccharine (sweetener)	954
Saffron or Crocetin or Crocin (colour)	164
Shellac (glazing agent)	904
Silicon dioxide, amorphous (anti-caking agent)	551
Silver (colour)	174
Sodium acetates (acidity regulator)	262
Sodium alginate (thickener, stabiliser, gelling agent)	401
Sodium aluminium phosphate (acidity regulator, emulsifier)	541
Sodium aluminosilicate (anti-caking agent)	554
Sodium ascorbate (antioxidant)	301
Sodium benzoate (preservative)	211
Sodium bisulphite (preservative)	222
Sodium carbonate or Sodium bicarbonate (acidity regulator, raising agent, anti-caking agent)	500
Sodium carboxymethylcellulose (thickener, stabiliser)	466
Sodium citrates (acidity regulator, emulsifier, stabiliser)	331
Sodium erythorbate (antioxidant)	316
Sodium ferrocyanide (anti-caking agent)	535
Sodium fumarate (acidity regulator)	365
Sodium lactate (acidity regulator, humectant, bulking agent)	325
Sodium lactylate or sodium oleyl lactylate or sodium stearoyl lactylate (emulsifier, stabiliser)	481
Sodium malates (acidity regulator, humectant)	350
Sodium metabisulphite (preservative)	223
Sodium nitrate (preservative, colour fixative)	251
Sodium nitrite (preservative, colour fixative)	250
Sodium phosphates (acidity regulator, emulsifier, stabiliser)	339
Sodium propionate (preservative)	281

Sodium sorbate (preservative)	201
Sodium sulphate (acidity regulator)	514
Sodium sulphite (preservative)	221
Sodium tartrates (acidity regulator)	335
Sorbic acid (preservative)	200
Sorbitan monostearate (emulsifier)	491
Sorbitan tristearate (emulsifier)	492
Sorbitol or sorbitol syrup (sweetener, humectant, emulsifier)	420
Stannous chloride (antioxidant)	512
Starch acetate esterified with acetic anhydride (thickener, stabiliser)	1420
Starch sodium octenylsuccinate (thickener, stabiliser)	1450
Stearic acid or fatty acid (glazing agent, foaming agent)	570
Succinic acid (acidity regulator)	363
Sucralose (sweetener)	955
Sucrose acetate isobutyrate (emulsifier, stabiliser)	444
Sucrose esters of fatty acids (emulsifier)	473
Sulphur dioxide (preservative)	220
Sunset yellow FCF (colour)	110
Tannic acid or tannins (colour, emulsifier, stabiliser, thickener)	181
Tartaric acid (acidity regulator, antioxidant)	334
Tartrazine (colour)	102
tert-Butylhydroquinone (antioxidant)	319
Thaumatin (flavour enhancer, sweetener)	957
Titanium dioxide (colour)	171
alpha -Tocopherol (antioxidant)	307
delta -Tocopherol (antioxidant)	309
gamma -Tocopherol (antioxidant)	308
Tocopherols concentrate, mixed (antioxidant)	306

Tragacanth gum (thickener, stabiliser)	413
Triacetin (humectant)	1518
Triethyl citrate (antifoaming agent)	1505
Violoxanthin (colour)	161e
Xanthan gum (thickener, stabiliser)	415
Xylitol (sweetener, humectant, stabiliser)	967

References

The author gratefully acknowledges the following sources of reference used in researching and compiling this book. Whilst every attempt has been made to trace and acknowledge copyright of all sources, if any sources have not been acknowledged, Additive Alert would be pleased to hear from the copyright owners so any omission can be rectified.

Books

Borushek Allan; *Allan Borushek's Pocket Calorie and Fat Counter*; Family Health Publications, WA Australia 2002

Buist Robert; *Food Sensitivity*; Harper and Row Publishers, NSW Australia 1986

Davis Damien; *Are You Poisoning Your Family*; Lamont Publishing, VIC Australia 1992

Dengate Sue; *Fed Up With Asthma*; Random House Australia, NSW Australia 2003

Dengate Sue; *Fed Up;* Random House Australia, NSW Australia 1998

Dingle Peter, Brown Toni; *Cosmetics and Personal Care Dangerous Beauty*; 1999

Dingle Peter, Brown Toni; *Sick Homes Part 1: Volatile Chemicals*; 1999

Dingle Peter; *The DEAL for Happier, Healthier, Smarter Kids*; 2004

Epstein Samuel S; *Unreasonable Risk*; Environmental Toxicology, Illinois USA 2002

Fisher Jo; *Food for Thought*; Heinemann Library 1997

Food Standards Australia New Zealand; *Food Additives and Labels*; Murdoch Books, NSW Australia 2002

FSANZ, *Benzene in flavoured Beverages*; June 2006

Hanssen Maurice; *The New Additive Code Breaker*; Lothian Books, VIC Australia 1989

Hermanussen and others, *Obesity, voracity and short stature: the impact of glutamate on the regulation of appetite*, Eur J Clii Nutr 2005

Jeffreys Toni Ph.D; *Your Health At Risk;* Thorsons; 1999

Lau K and others, *Synergistic Interactions between Commonly used Food Additives in a Developmental Neurotoxicity Test*, Toxicol Sci 2005 Dec 13

Millstone Eric, Abraham John; *ADDITIVES A Guide for Everyone;* Penquin Books, London 1988

Pleshette Janet; *Health On Your Plate*; Arrow Books, London 1983

Simontacchi Carol; *The Crazy Makers: How the Food Industry is Destroying Our Brains and Harming Our Children*; Penquin Putnam Inc, New York USA 2000

Statham Bill; *The Chemical Maze 2nd Edition*; POSSIBILITY. COM, VIC Australia 2002

Treffers Sue; *Food Additives Pocket Reference Series*; Mastercorp Pty Ltd, QLD Australia 2003

Internet sources

About Asthma; Asthma Australia;
www.asthmaaustralia.org.au/asthma

ADD and Diet; A Current Affair Factsheet 25 April 2000;
www.ninemsn.com.au

Chemical Cuisine CSPI's Guide to Food Additives; Centre for
Science in the Public Interest;
www.cspinet.orgreports/chemcuisine

*Chemicals combine in our bodies but are rarely tested that
way. Why?;* Centre for Children's Health and the
Environment, Mount Sinai School of Medicine;
www.childenvironment.org

Do Food Additives Subtract from Health?; Business Week;
www.businessweek.com/1996

Food Additives Guide; www.foodag.com

*Food Additives- What you always wanted to know about food
additives but had no one to ask*; Food Allergy Centre;
www.x-sitez.com/allergy/additives

Food Additives: Are they making us sick?; A Current Affair
Factsheet 17 January 2002; www.ninemsn.com.au

Food Additives: Common Types; A Current Affair Factsheet 17
January 2002; www.ninemsn.com.au

Food Additives; BBC News 6 October 1999 Health Medical
Notes; www.news.bbc.co.uk

Food Additives; Food Standards Australia New Zealand;
www.foodstandards.gov.au

Food Additives; Nutrition Australia;
www.nutritionaustralia.org/Food_Facts/FAQ

Food Additives–detailed list of effects; Quackbusters; www.quackbusters.com.au/food_additives

Food Allergy or Food Intolerance?; Food Intolerance Network Factsheet; www.fedupwithfoodadditives.info/factsheets

Food: Food Safety Food Additives; Choice; www.choice.au/articles

Gold Mark D; *Monosodium Glutamate (MSG);* www.holisticmed.com/msg

Gold Mark D; *The Bitter Truth About Artificial Sweeteners*; Extracted from Nexus Magazine Volume 2/ 28 and Volume 3/1; www.nexusmagazine.com/Aspartame

Goodspeed Michael; *Processed Foods May Damage the Developing Brain*; 1999; www.rense.com/health3

Guide to Food Additives; Food Allergy Centre; www.x-sitez.com/allergy/additives

Haas Elson MD; *Food Additives and Human Health*; (Extract from Staying Healthy Shopper's Guide: Feed Your Family Safely; Healthy Child online; www.healthychild.com

Johnny can't read, sit still or stop hitting the neighbour's kid. Why?; Centre for Children's Health and the Environment, Mount Sinai School of Medicine; www.childenvironment.org

List of substances scheduled for evaluation or re-evaluation; Joint FAO/WHO Expert Committee on Food Additives (JECFA) Sixty First meeting Rome, 10–19 June 2003; www.x-sitez.com/allergy/additives/vege400-495

More Kids Are Getting Brain Cancer. Why?; Centre for Children's Health and the Environment, Mount Sinai School of Medicine; www.childenvironment.org

Our most precious natural resource is being threatened. Why?; Centre for Children's Health and the Environment, Mount Sinai School of Medicine; www.childenvironment.org

Pesticides could become the ultimate male contraceptive. Why?; Centre for Children's Health and the Environment, Mount Sinai School of Medicine; www.childenvironment.org

Schardt David; *Diet and Behaviour in Children*; Nutrition Action Newsletter March 2000; www.cspinet.org/nah

She's the test subject for thousands of toxic chemicals. Why?; Centre for Children's Health and the Environment, Mount Sinai School of Medicine; www.childenvironment.org

Splenda Information Sheet; Sucralose Toxicity Information Centre; www.holisticmed.com/splenda

The Bread Preservative (282); Food Intolerance Network Factsheet; www.fedupwithfoodadditives.info/factsheets

The Hyperactive Children's Support Group; www.hacsg.org.uk

Trouble may begin in the grocery cart; Feingold Association of the United States; www.feingold.org

Press and media articles

Arma Ingrid; *My sandwich is toxic*; The Sunday Times, 8 September 2002

Asthma fight stepped up; The West Australian, 26 August 2002

Dalton Rodney; *Waistline deadline*; The Weekend Australian, 22 June 2002

Frozen fat the choice in chips; The West Australian, 9 September 2003

Healthy Scepticism; The Weekend Australian, 5 July 2003

James Amanda; *WA Top state for 'dexies'*; The West Australian, 4 September 2002

James Amanda; *WA youth taller but much fatter*; The West Australian, 11 September 2002

Laurie Victoria; *A battle plan to save the children of a 'toxic society'*; The Australian, 2002

Laurie Victoria; *The Hyper State*; The Weekend Australian Magazine, 8 February 2003

McKimmie Marnie; *Depression food link raised*; The West Australian, 11 February 2004

Milburn Caroline; *Children in crisis: expert*; The West Australian, 9 November 2002

Miller Margaret; *Busy teens grab junk food*; The West Australian, 25 June 2003

O'Leary Cathy; *Asthma record among the worst;* The West Australian, 6 May 2004

O'Leary Cathy; *Diabetes alert for obese children*; The West Australian, 5 May 2004

O'Leary Cathy; *New wave of young diabetics*; The West Australian, 25 November 2003

O'Leary Cathy; *Not so sweet findings for additive*; The West Australian, 10 May 2004

Pemble Lousie; *Forget the gimmicks and go back to basics*; The Weekend Australian, 5 July 2003

Rasdien Peta; *Warnings on high-fat food wanted: survey*; The West Australian, 22 July 2003

Rose Rebecca; *Ban junk food ads: expert*; The West Australian, 11 September 2002

Stanton Dr Rosemary; *Chewing the Fat*; Australian Good Taste Magazine; September 2003

Miscellaneous sources

Butylated Hydroxyanisole(BHA) CAS No. 25013-16-5; *Reasonably Anticipated to be a Carcinogen*; Ninth Report on Carcinogens.

Dingle Peter; *2600 Food Additives Course Notes*; July 2003

J Breaky; Review Article - *The role of diet and behaviour in childhood;* Journal of Paediatrics and Child Health 1997;33 (3):190-4

Lau K and others; *Synergistic Interactions Between Commonly Used Food Additives in a Developmental Neurotoxicity Test;* Toxicol Sci 2005: Dec 13

Hermanussen and others; *Obesity, voracity and short stature: the impact of glutamate on the regulation of appetite*; European Journal of Clinical Nutrition, 2005

Bateman B and others; *The effects of a double blind, placebo controlled artificial food colourings and benzoate preservatives challenge on hyperactivity in a general population sample of pre school children*; Archives of Diseases in Childhood 2004; 899: 506 -511

Mc Cann D and others; *Food additives and hyperactive behaviour in 3-year-old and 8/9-year-old children in the community: a randomised, double-blinded, placebo-controlled trial*; The Lancet Vol 370, Issue 9598, 3 November 2007, Pages 1560 – 1567

Piper PW; *Yeast superoxide dismutase mutants reveal a pro-oxidant action of weak organic acid food preservatives;* Free Radic Biol Med. 1999 Dec;27(11-12):1219-27. PMID: 10641714

Mr Steve McCutcheon
CEO, Food Standards Australia New Zealand
PO Box 7186
CANBERRA ACT 2610

Dear Mr McCutcheon,

RE: Full disclosure of ingredients

I am writing to you as a concerned consumer who has recently become aware of serious shortcomings in our food-labelling code administered by your agency. My understanding is that, despite the recent changes to the labelling requirements in this country, there still exists a 5% loophole that enables manufacturers to not disclose fully the ingredients in their products. The current legislation allows for manufacturers not to declare components of ingredients that make up less than 5% of a product or which are determined by the manufacturer as having no technological function.

As a result of this loophole, there are many products on the market that contain food additives that are, quite legally, not declared on the label. Consumers are consequently denied the right to be fully informed about what is in the food we eat. For whatever reasons, many consumers wish to avoid certain substances, and the current legislation doesn't support the consumers' right to full information and choice. Rather, it appears biased in favour of manufacturers.

As the charter of FSANZ is to protect the health and safety of people, I believe that your agency has a clear responsibility to ensure that full-disclosure in labelling is introduced without delay.

Consumers have a right to know what is in the food we purchase, regardless of whether or not additives are deemed safe. It is the responsibility of FSANZ to ensure that the labelling legislation in this country is amended to reflect this change and to require that manufacturers declare all components of their products, no matter how small or what function they are deemed to perform.

Thank you for your consideration of this issue. I look forward to hearing from you regarding the timing for such changes to be implemented by your agency.

Yours sincerely,

....

Some comments from our readers

Since Additive Alert was published in September 2004, we have been inundated with confirmation from all over the country that food additives are playing havoc with the health and well being of Australians, both young and old. Additive Alert does not make any specific health claims, nor do we promise a miracle cure for any health or behaviour problems. However, the anecdotal evidence we receive from everyday real people is undeniably strong. Food additives and diet can play a huge role in alleviating problems for many people.

Here is a small sample of what people have to say about the way food additives effect them and how Additive Alert has helped them. I hope this book will help you too.

****

"I bought your book because my nearly two year old (girl) was such a terrible night time sleeper that I no longer knew what to do with her. So out went the additives and preservatives, along came my bookmark when I went shopping and we began making all our own treats, cakes and biscuits. What a difference it made!!!. My 31/2 year old (girl) does not seem to have any of the same issues with much of the food although I did notice the change in their aggressive behaviour within days. Thank you so much."

****

"As a mother of three I have tried to maintain what I thought was a healthy diet for my kids since they were born, insisting on fresh fruit and vegetables and little to no junk food. However, a friend recently bought your book and I was shocked to say the least at how little I really knew, and I was outraged at the fact that FSANZ is basically using our children as guinea pigs. I am sending this email to say THANKYOU for all the hard work and thank you for making me aware of what they put in our food."

****

" My life has been totally transformed since cutting out foods which I thought would be ok even though I knew they would not be of any nutritional value. Its a big statement to say that "I have got my life back" but that is what has happened since I avoided foods containing the worst additives. It is nearly criminal what is being given to us in the name of food. Please put me on your data base."